You look better online

EMMET TRUXES

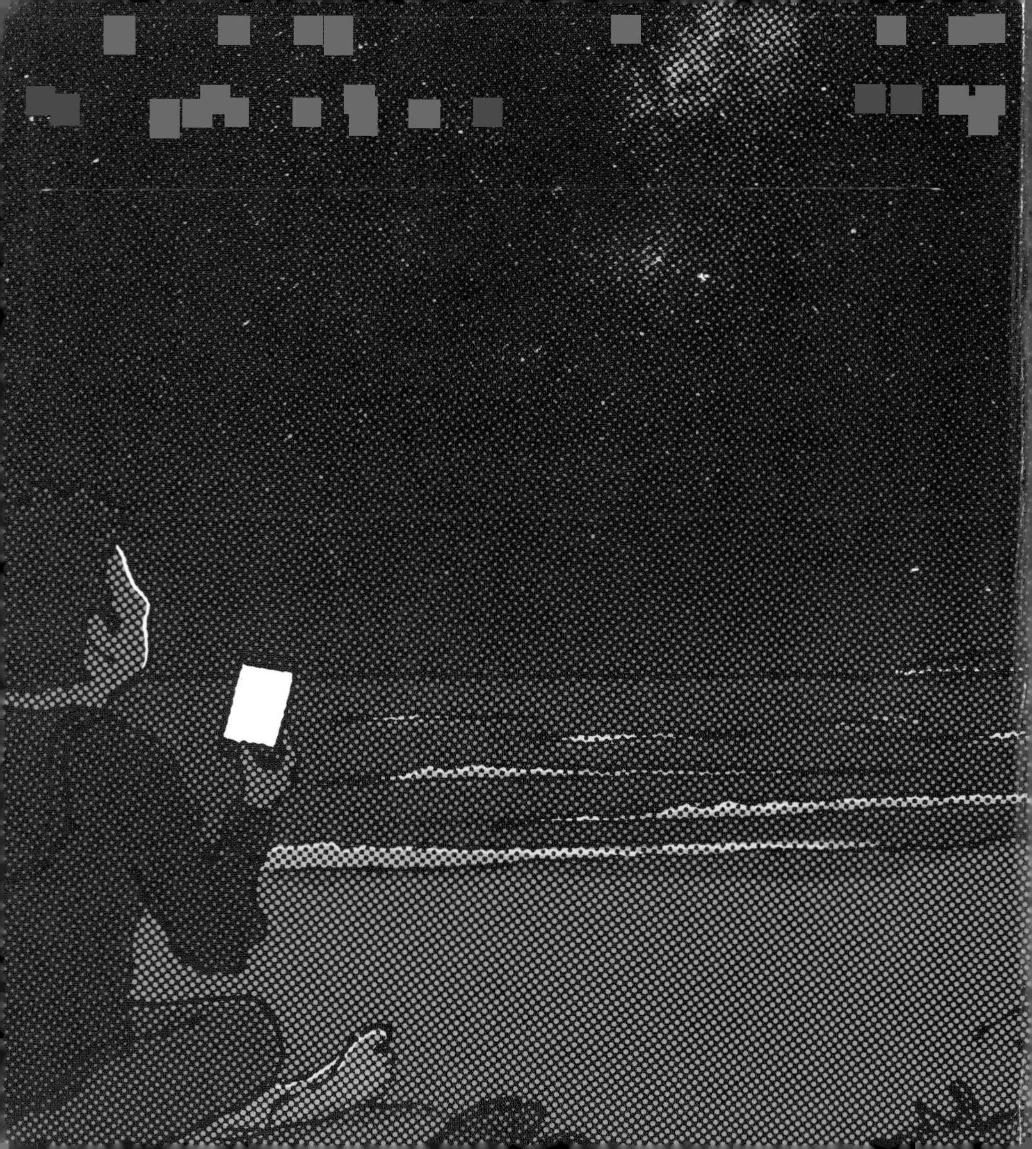

You look better online

EMMET TRUXES

ABRAMS, NEW YORK

Editor: Samantha Weiner
Designer: Devin Grosz
Production Manager: Rebecca Westall

Library of Congress Control Number: 2017930300

ISBN: 978-1-4197-2640-8

Printed and bound in China
10 9 8 7 6 5 4 3 2 1

Abrams books are available at special discounts when
purchased in quantity for premiums and promotions as well
as fundraising or educational use. Special editions can also be
created to specification. For details, contact specialsales@
abramsbooks.com or the address below.

ABRAMS The Art of Books
115 West 18th Street, New York, NY 10011
abramsbooks.com

Introduction

You look better online. Now quick, react to that with only one emoji!

Impossible, right? I'd need at least twenty. Put simply, the relationship we have with the Internet—and especially those tiny computers we keep in our pockets and purses—is a complicated one. It's no stretch to say that we are flying at warp speed through the peaks and valleys of digital addiction. And there is no end in sight.

Here's something I find incredible. This planet is *googles discreetly* 4.543 billion years old, and you and I just happen to exist at a specific moment when exponential technological progress is rapidly connecting humanity and changing every single aspect of our interactions. For all the messiness, it's clearly an amazing time to be alive.

This book is a series of reflections about this moment told from the perspective of my generation. I'm a millennial—one of the twenty- and thirty-somethings currently trekking through the early years of adulthood, smartphone in hand. We drink straight from the fire-hose of our feeds, obsessing over our online image—swiping, scrolling, tweeting, liking, and snapping from one dopamine hit to the next. We played a vital role in shaping this futuristic present, and we're the last generation that will ever remember a staticky childhood without the Internet, social media, or smartphones.

I drew all the time as a kid, creating my own worlds on paper. When I first started cartooning in college, smartphones didn't exist. I inked and washed everything on watercolor board, scanned and edited in Photoshop, and emailed the finished file to my editor to be printed days later. Now, I've switched to drawing everything with a digital pencil on an art tablet. Within minutes of finishing an illustration, I post it on Instagram and it immediately shows up in the hands of my followers. That's it. It never ceases to blow my mind.

If you're seeing my cartoons for the first time, welcome, I hope you like what you find! If you've been following @brooklyncartoons on Insta, then I'd like to congratulate you for not being on your phone right now! Honestly, I'm immeasurably humbled that you hit that follow button and in no small way helped make this book a reality. It's beyond cool that what started as a purely digital, fun side project could generate this very tangible artifact.

And so, as we begin, I wish you all the following: May your journey through life be #blessed with high engagement, perfect selfie light, and strong Wi-Fi. And may the algorithms be ever in your favor.

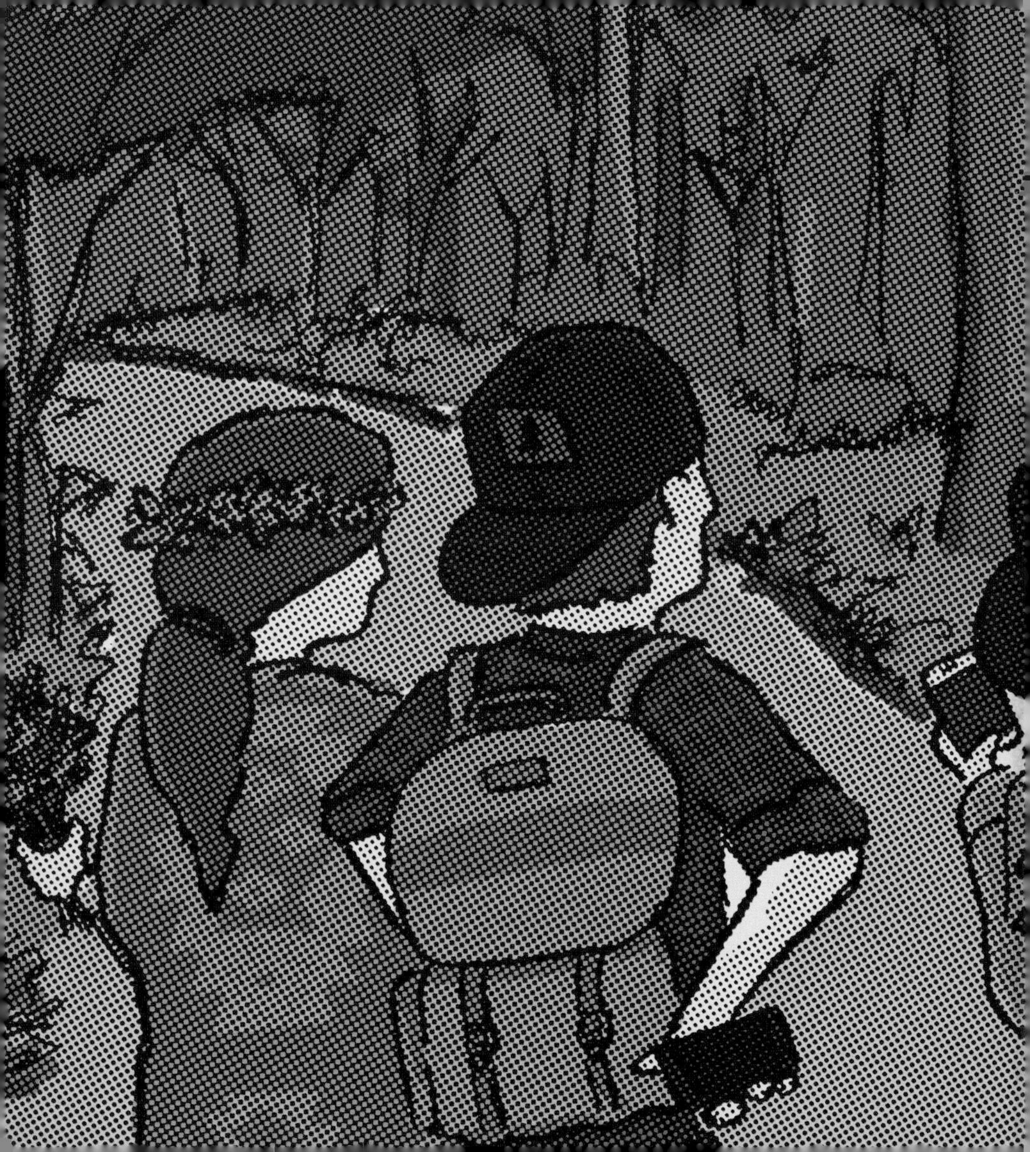

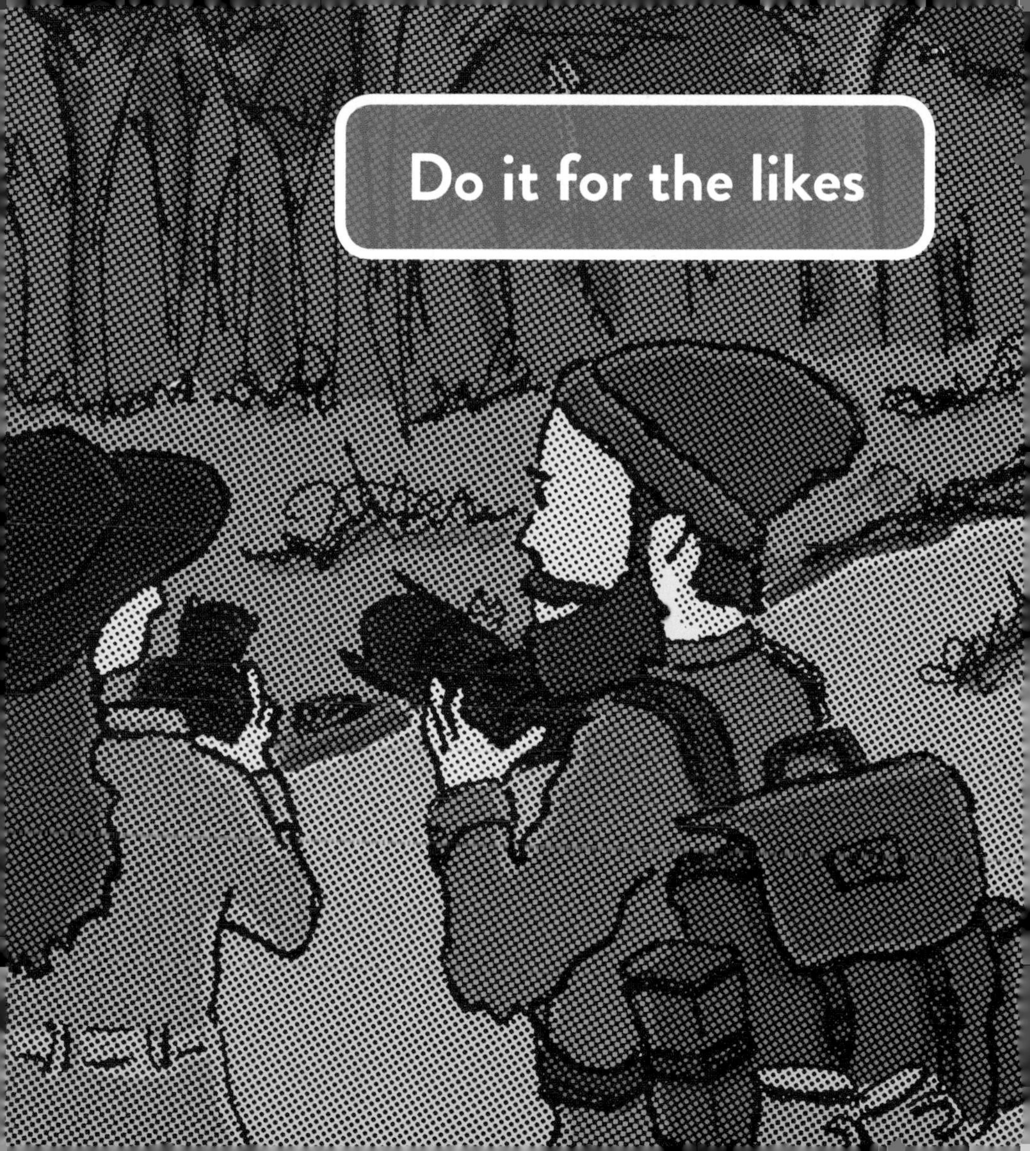
Do it for the likes

"Babe, it needs to look more spontaneous."

"*Does the pork belly photograph well?*"

"Your father and I noticed you haven't posted to social media in over a week. Please call us."

"You can follow the play-by-play on my Snap story."

Girl: If I suddenly died I'd want my last Instagram to reflect me accurately and not just be something trivial.

Friend: Yeah, I posted latte art today. That would be too sad.

*Facebook: where your sloppy seconds
are other people's soulmates.*

"He asked to sit alone so we wouldn't interrupt his tweetstorm."

"I just thought of a caption that's the perfect combination of witty and self-deprecating."

Father: You're so special, kiddo.

Daughter: Thanks, but if I've learned one thing from social media, it's that we're all unexceptional, unoriginal, and unremarkable. . .

"I deleted everything off my Instagram pre-mustache. It's off-brand at this point."

"I took two flights and one train for this. Now take it again!"

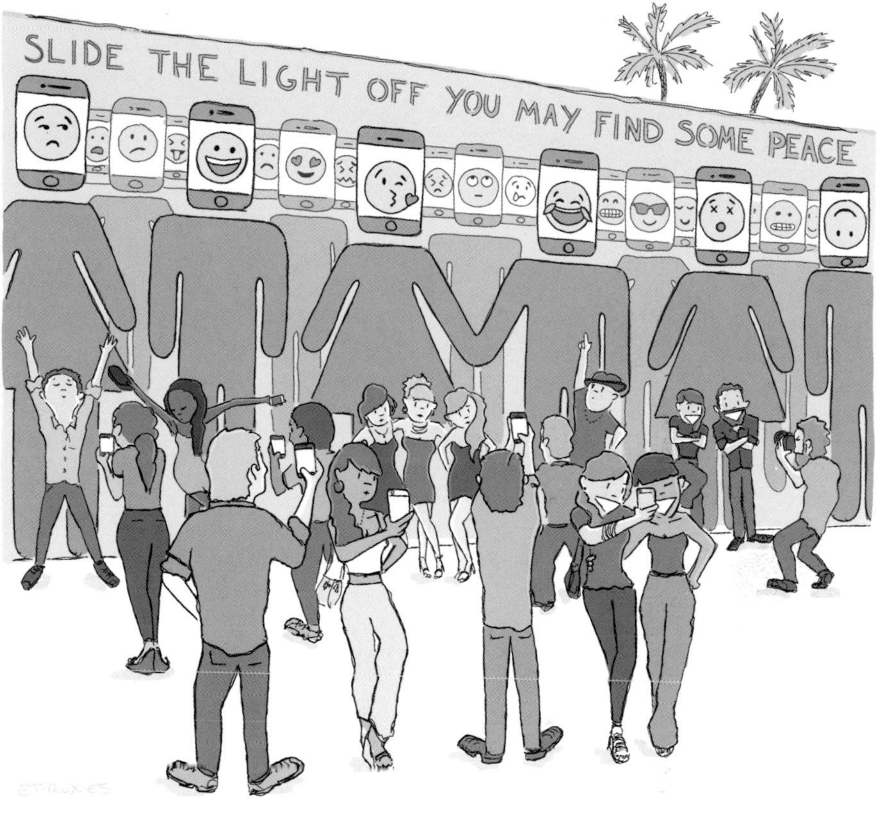
SLIDE THE LIGHT OFF YOU MAY FIND SOME PEACE

If a tree falls in the forest and no one 'grams it,
then clearly that tree didn't fall in the right place.

"Wait, you're broadcasting this live!?"

"You've been tweeting a lot of song lyrics lately."

Keeping up with the Kardashians.

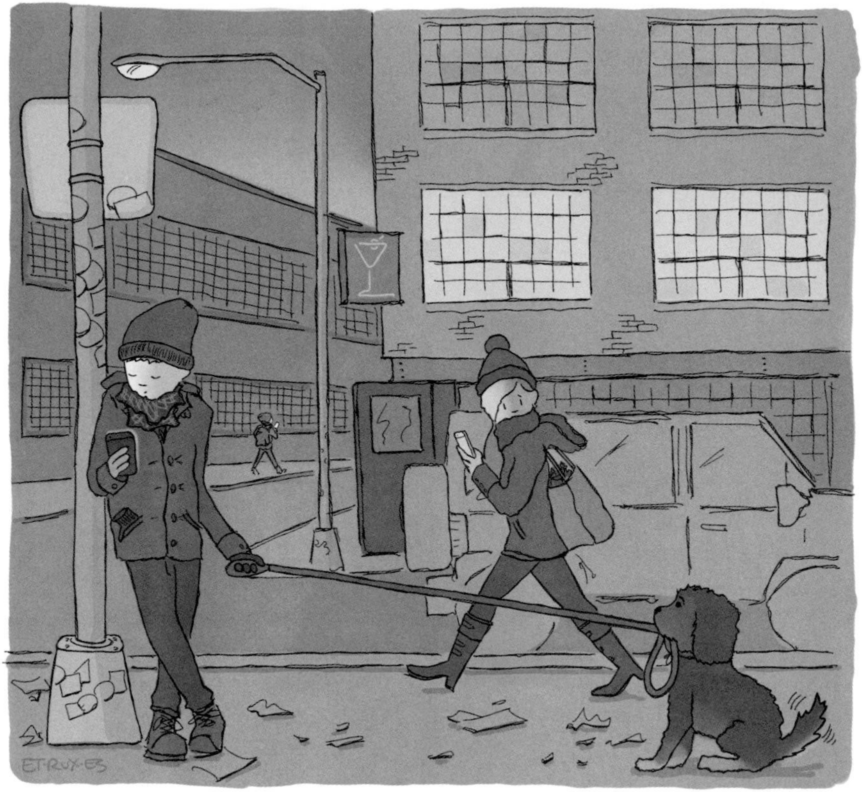

Late night scroll.

"Let's promise not to follow each other on social media so we can keep this friendship a pleasant memory."

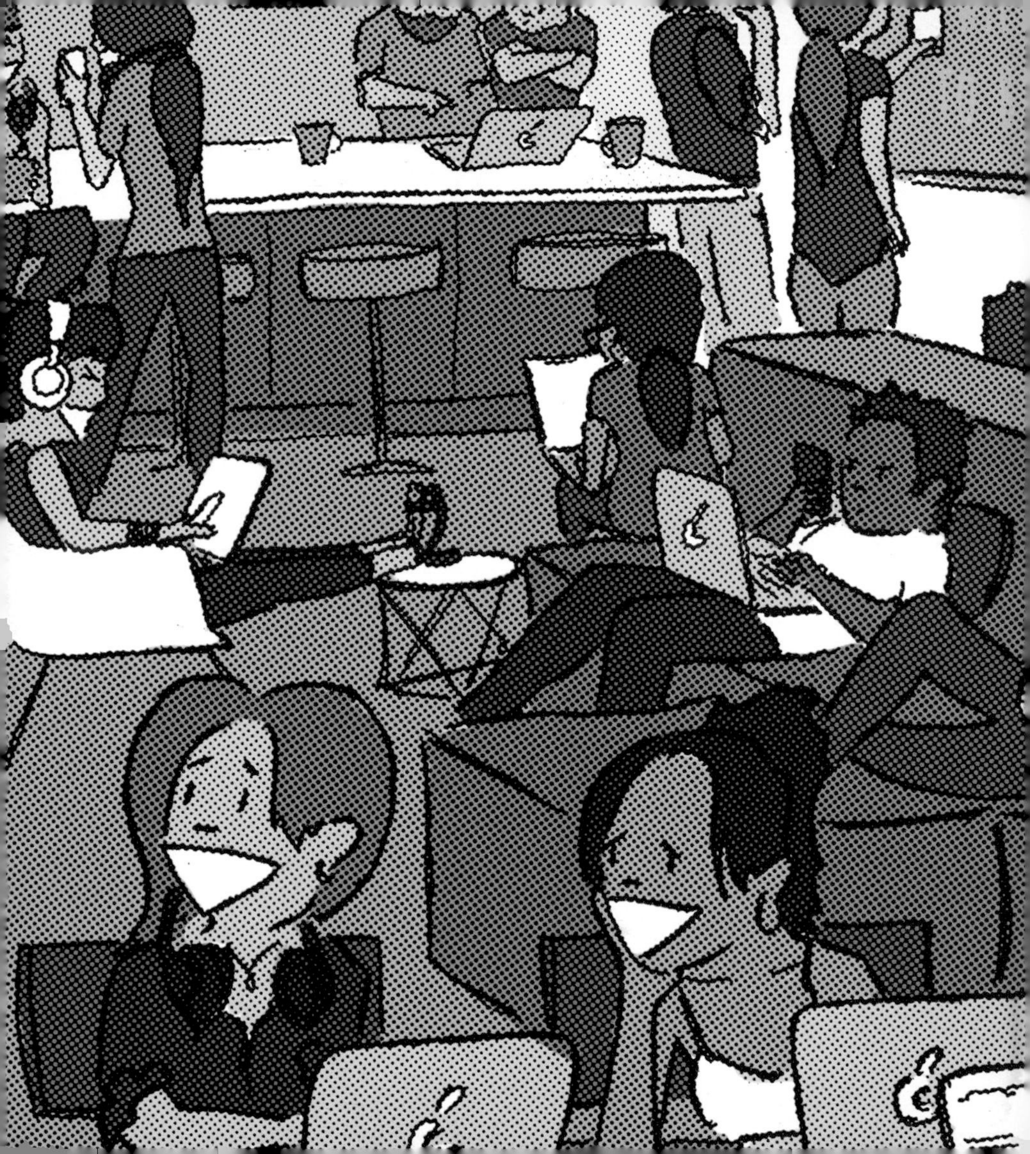

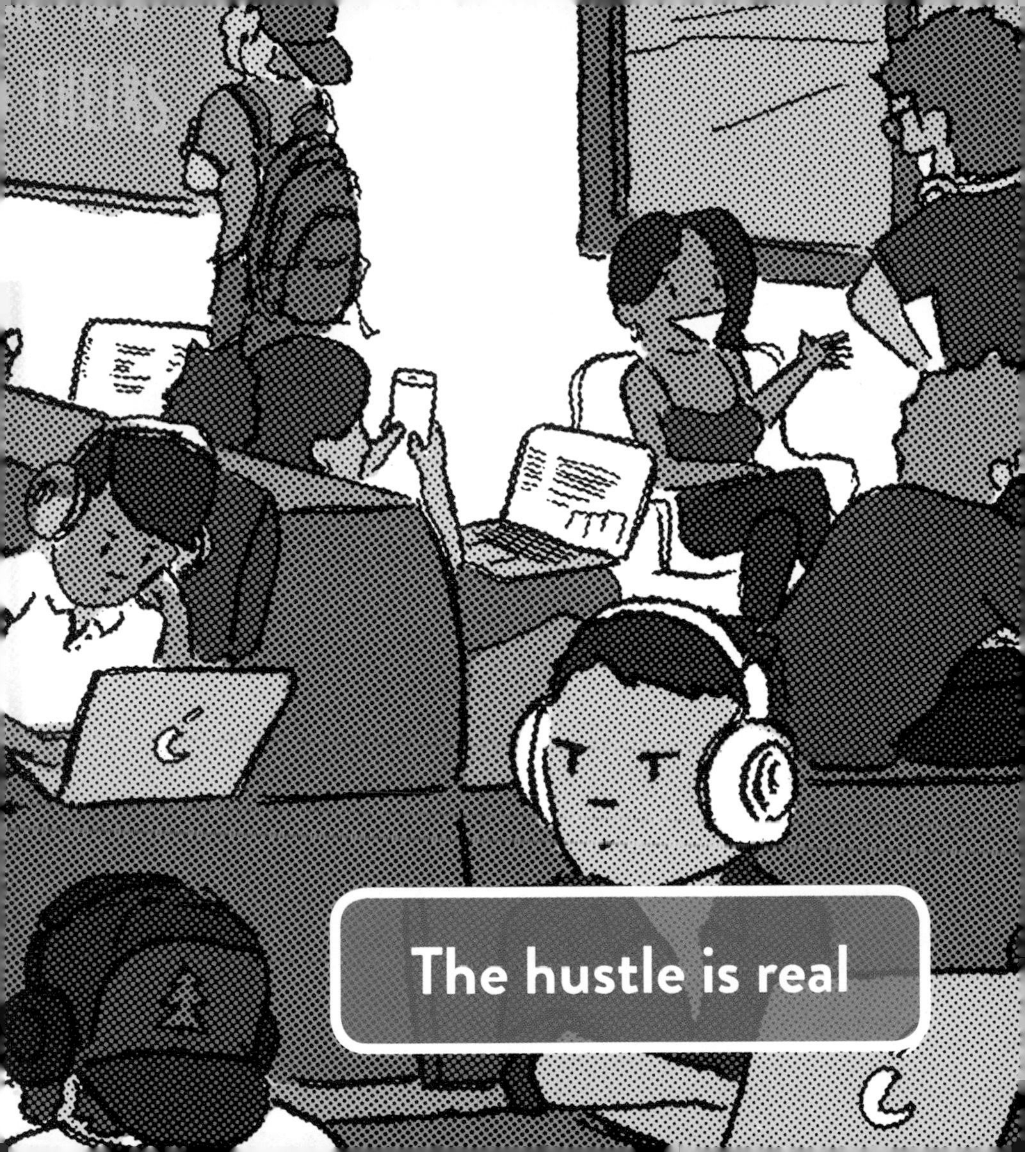
The hustle is real

"When I grow up, I want to be a brand!"

"My nutritionist says sitting is the new smoking."

And for what seemed like eternity, time stood still.

"They're good, but they're not 'startup good.'"

"This year for Halloween I'm gonna dress up as someone with a 9-5 job and scare the shit out of everyone in L.A."

@overheardla

"I'm an actor, writer, director, producer,
cinematographer, and I model."

Guy: So you're a blogger?

Girl: I prefer "Digital Content Architect."

@larkinclark

"This isn't an information business; this is an affirmation business. We tell our readers what they already know."

Girl 1: Excuse me, your phone is ringing.

Girl 2: If they really need me they'll text.

Meanwhile, in San Francisco . . .

"Oh, you're VP and a global head of something? Fascinating."

"Colin will happily be your unpaid intern for as long as it takes."

Reporter: So you're a successful entrepreneur, what advice do you have for the kids?

Entrepreneur: Don't give your fucks away. Monetize them.

"Sorry I'm late, the traffic this morning was ridiculous."

"I don't see the problem as long as the revenue is real."

*"If you can shut up about whatever app
you're developing, I'll buy your next round."*

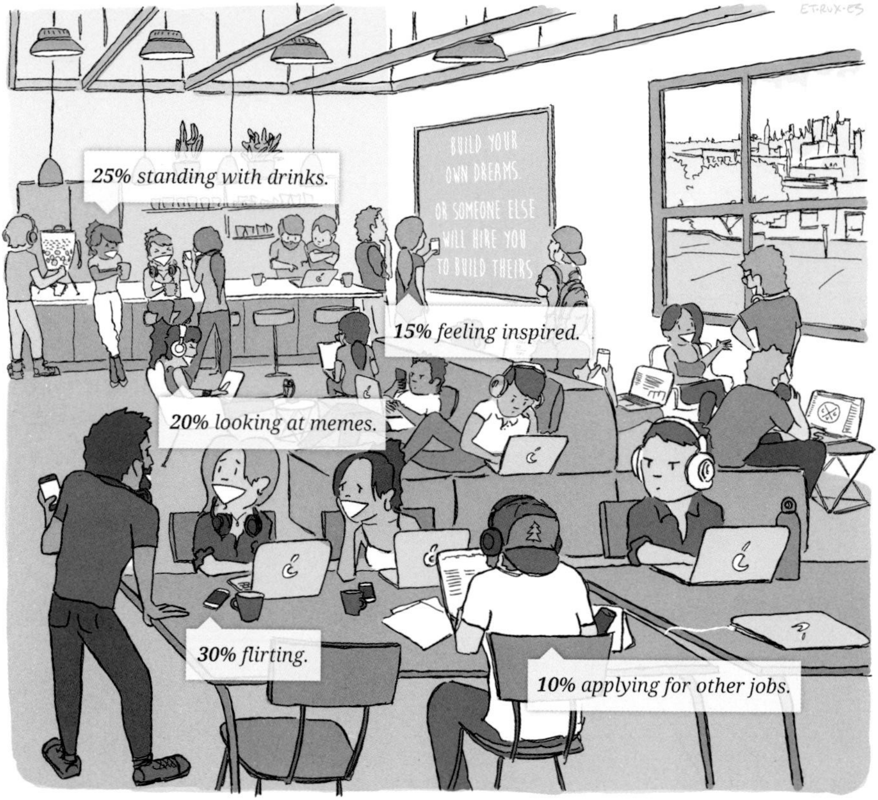
ET-RUX-ES
25% standing with drinks.
BUILD YOUR OWN DREAMS. OR SOMEONE ELSE WILL HIRE YOU TO BUILD THEIRS
15% feeling inspired.
20% looking at memes.
30% flirting.
10% applying for other jobs.

0% productivity.

"Fantastic, I'm penciling you in right now."

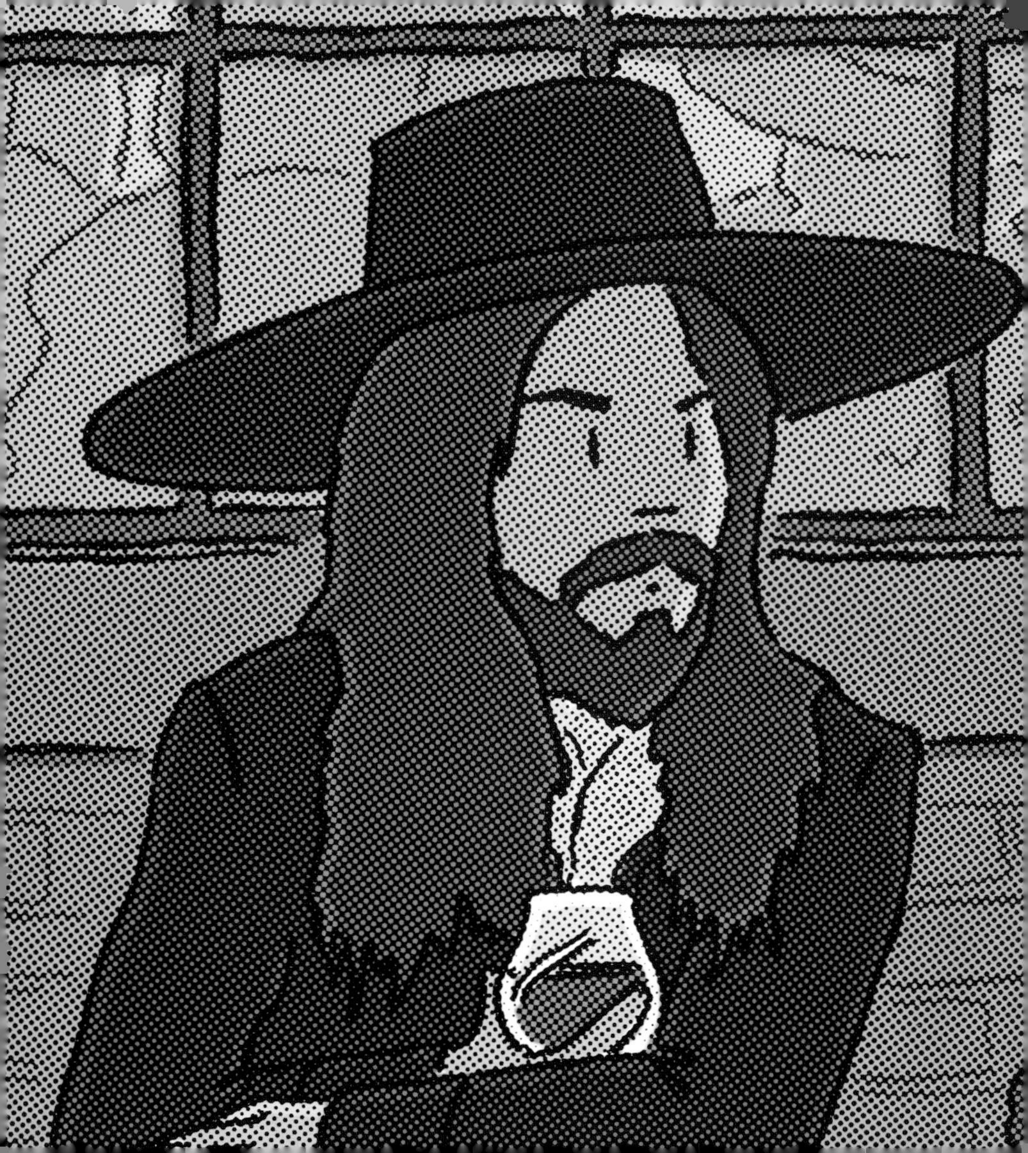

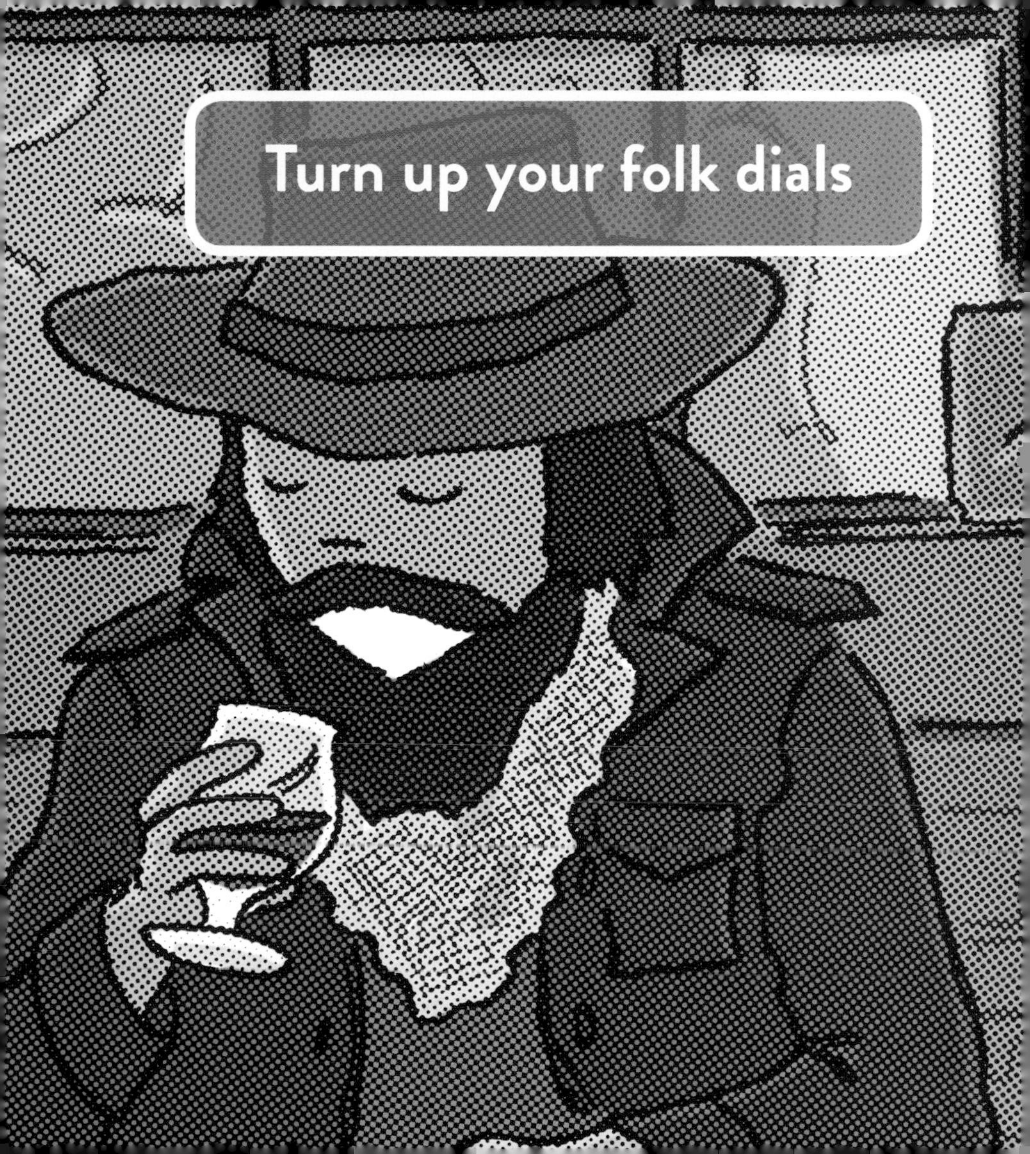
Turn up your folk dials

How to tie a perfect manbun.

In three simple steps.

Step 1.

Step 2.

Step 3.

"Which way is more aesthetically pleasing?"

"Could you bring the roasted beet salad as a juice?"

"*Dicen que están en 'wanderlust.'*"

In Hell, you have to be stuck in a room with one of these guys for all of eternity.

Which one do you choose?

"But they don't have slim fit."

"Excuse me . . . is that really your phone,
or are you part of the retro ambiance?"

I really hope they put a bar here.

A restaurant would be cool, too.

Any place where people can hang after a long day.

ET·RUX·ES

"I'll start with the Wi-Fi password."

Guy 1: Dude, check it out, I'm gonna start selling these cool geometric things that have air plants in them!

Guy 2: That got old a long time ago, are you sure you wanna—

Guy 1: Sorry bro, I can't hear you above all this creativity.

"Care to sample our artisanal toothpicks paired with a selection of local cheese?"

"Just move an inch or two closer to the edge."

Him: These prices are insane. Can we just go to Ikea?

Her: Nope. This is a part of growing up, get used to it.

Accessories sold separately.

Barista: French press or pour over?

Girl: Pou're.

Not Authentic

kinda authentic

AUTHENTIC

RUGGED+REFINED

THE MOST AUTHENTIC

///////// TRUSTED QUALITY /////////

*"I dig your concept, dude, but I think
my concept is more real than your concept."*

@bogartmypix

"And this is where we make everything look artisanal."

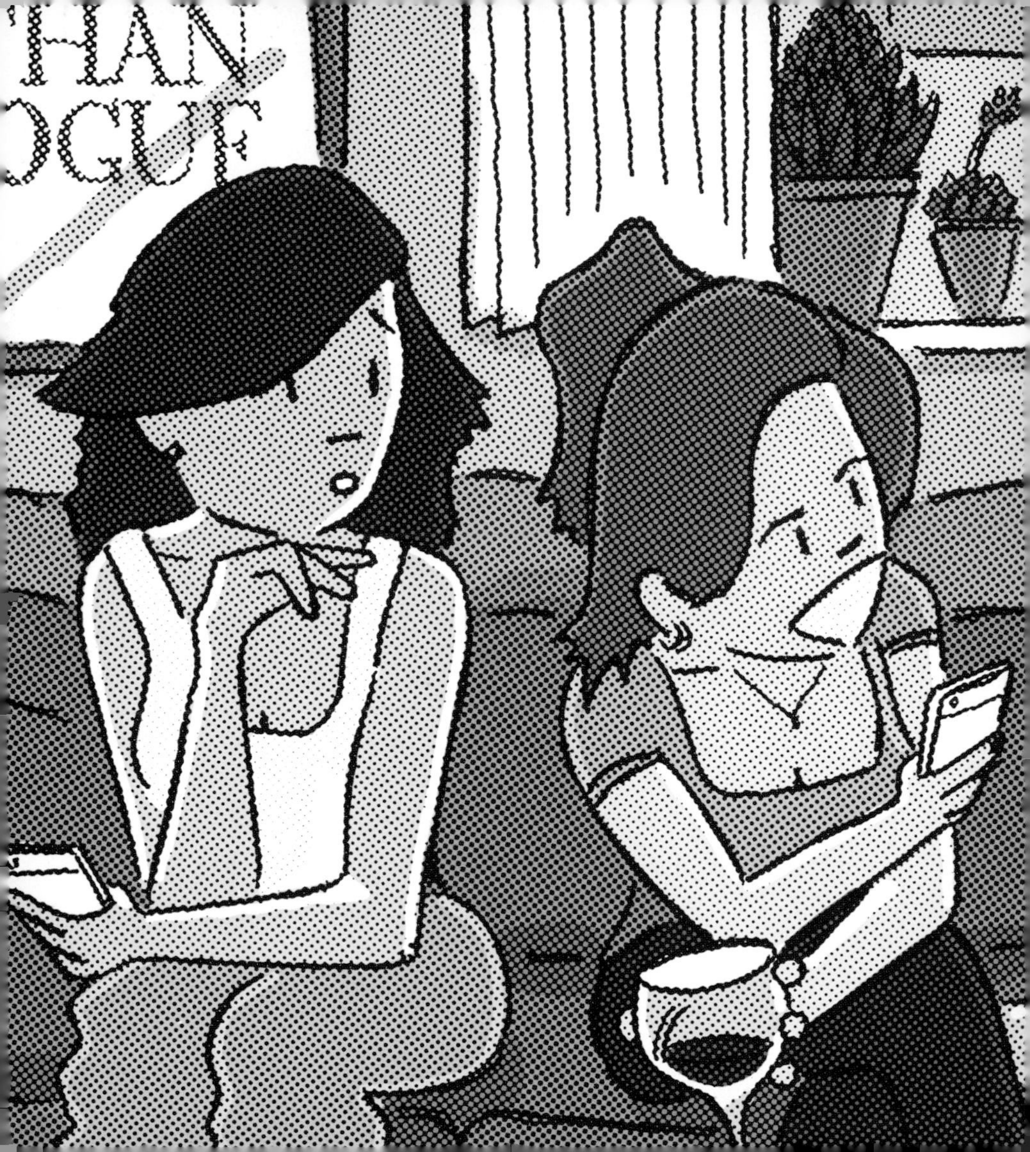

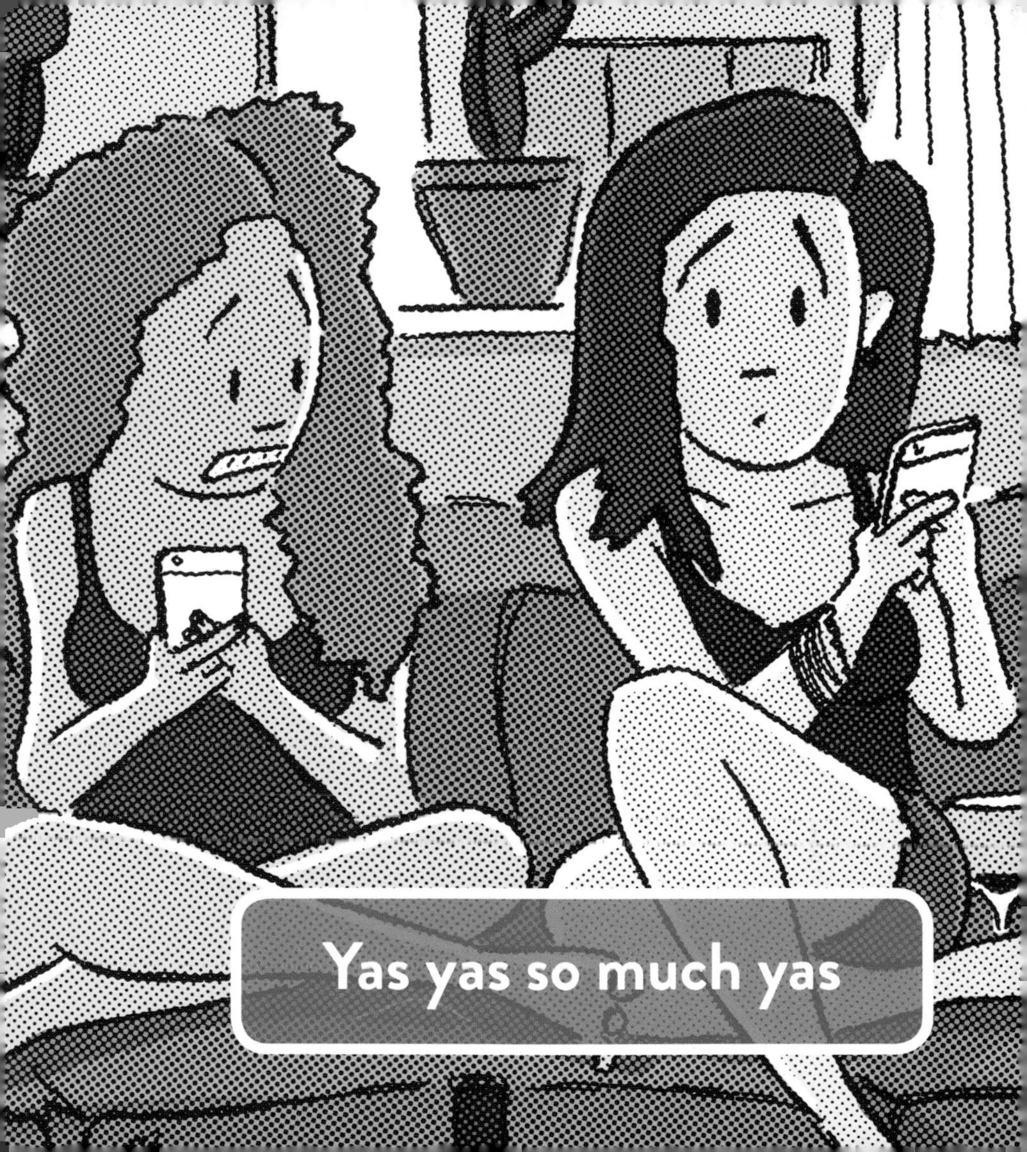
Yas yas so much yas

"False alarm. No one here is actually dying."

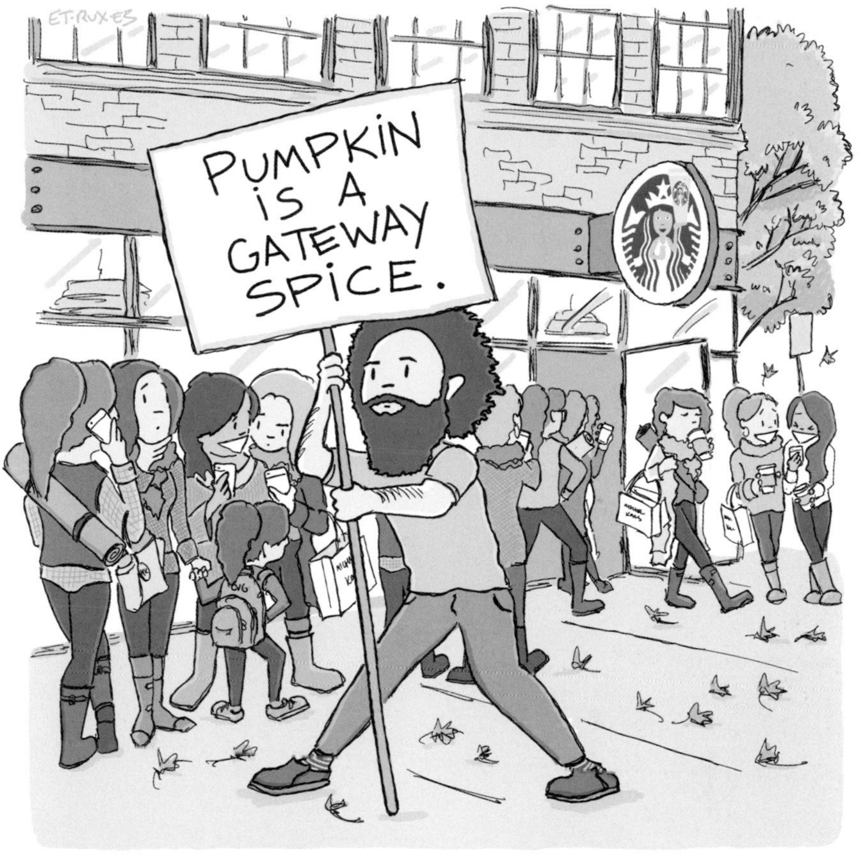
PUMPKIN IS A GATEWAY SPICE.
ET·RUX·ES

"But what if I'm from California?"

"To be honest, I think I've just been afraid of my own inner power."

Did someone just say music festivals?

Yas.   *Yaaaas.*   *Yaaaaaaaaaassssss.*

"I never told her, but I was always jealous of her resting bitch face."

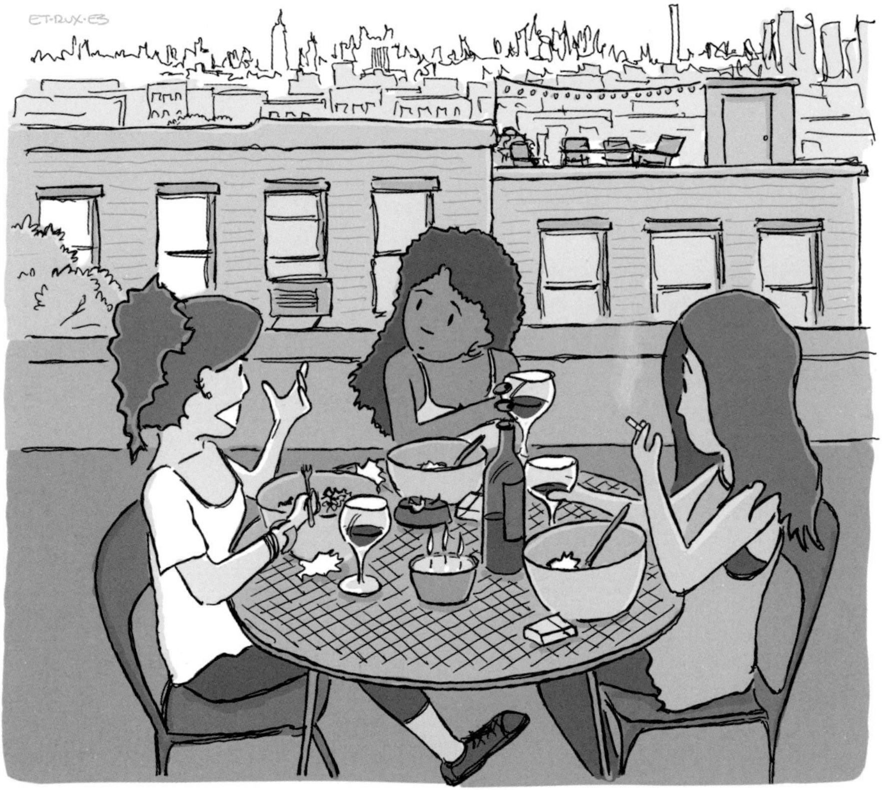

"Brittany? Oh my god, I hate Brittany so much! All she does is talk badly about people when they're not around."

Hell is taking group photos of five girls and then choosing one that everyone agrees on forever.

Girl 1: You two would really get along. She's just like you.

Girl 2: My serious side or my fun side?

"Guys, the best lighting in the apartment is actually up here."

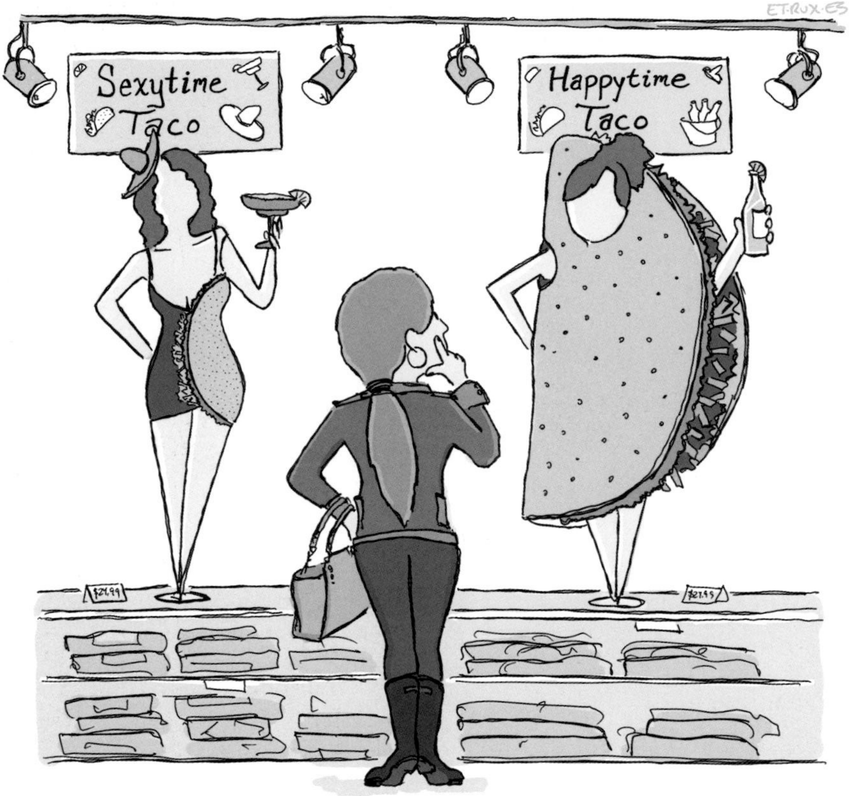
Sexytime Taco
Happytime Taco

"I am so much more humble than you."

Wednesdays.

@womenwholovewine

"Why did you just text me, Karen? I'm right here."

*"I really want to get along with my kid,
so maybe I should have a Libra baby."*

@overheardla

"I'm rolling my eyes so hard right now."

Man: Smile! You look upset.

Woman: That's just my face.

Every morning I say to my selfie, "Today I will even."

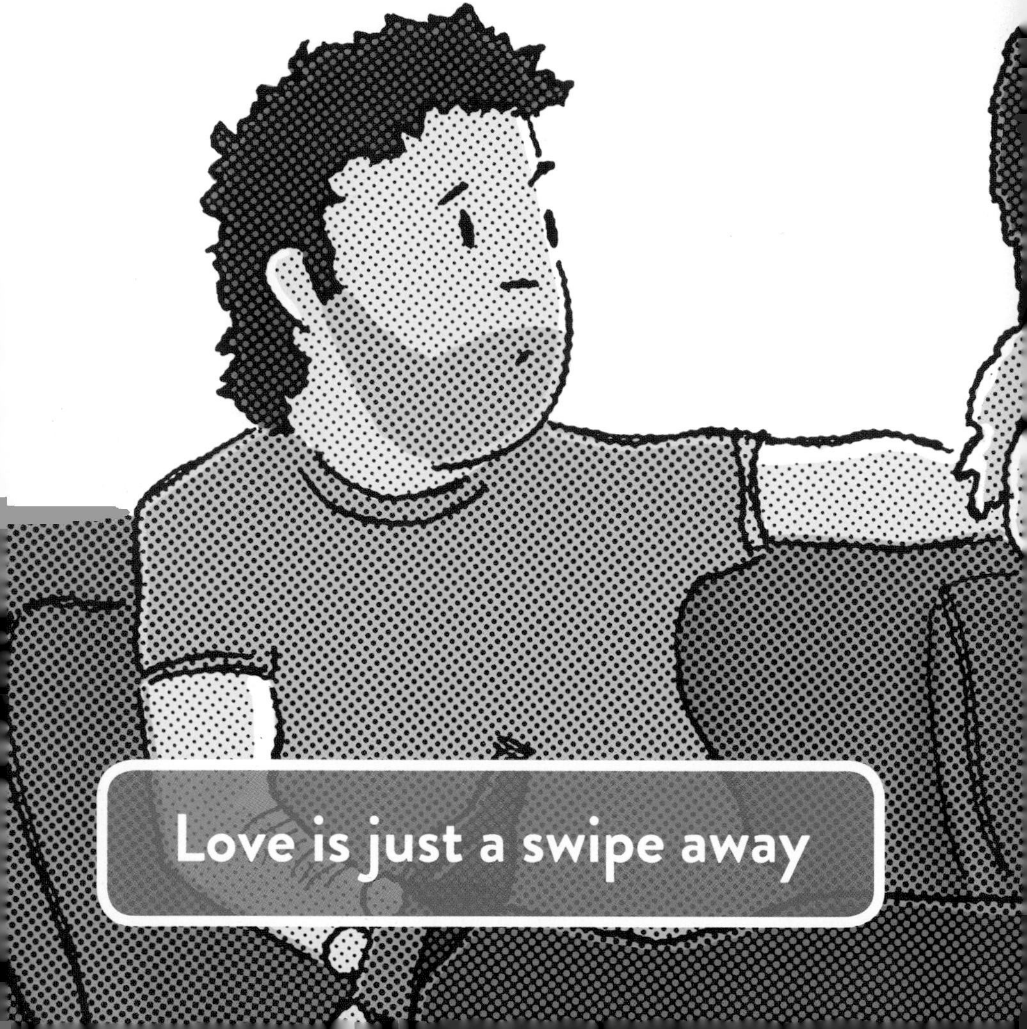
Love is just a swipe away

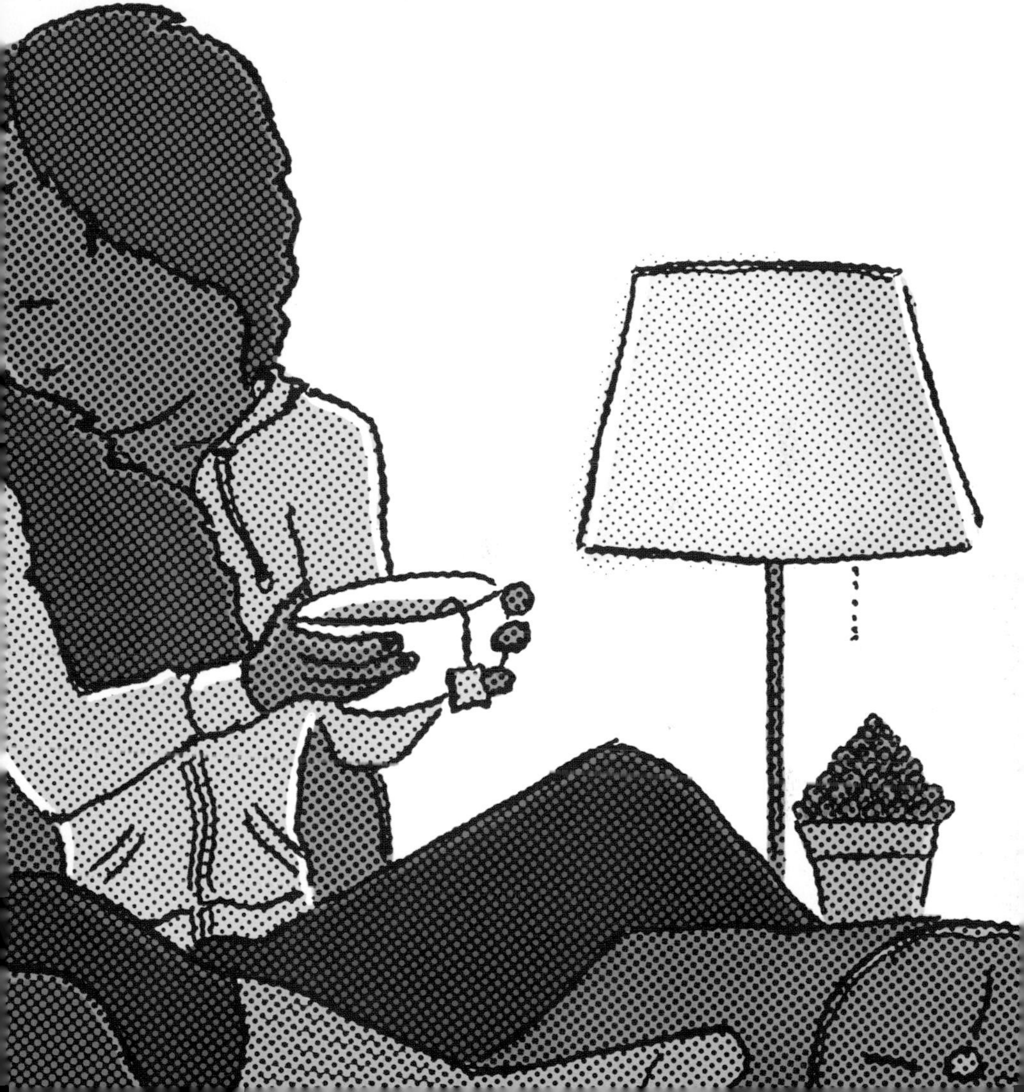

Do I like him?

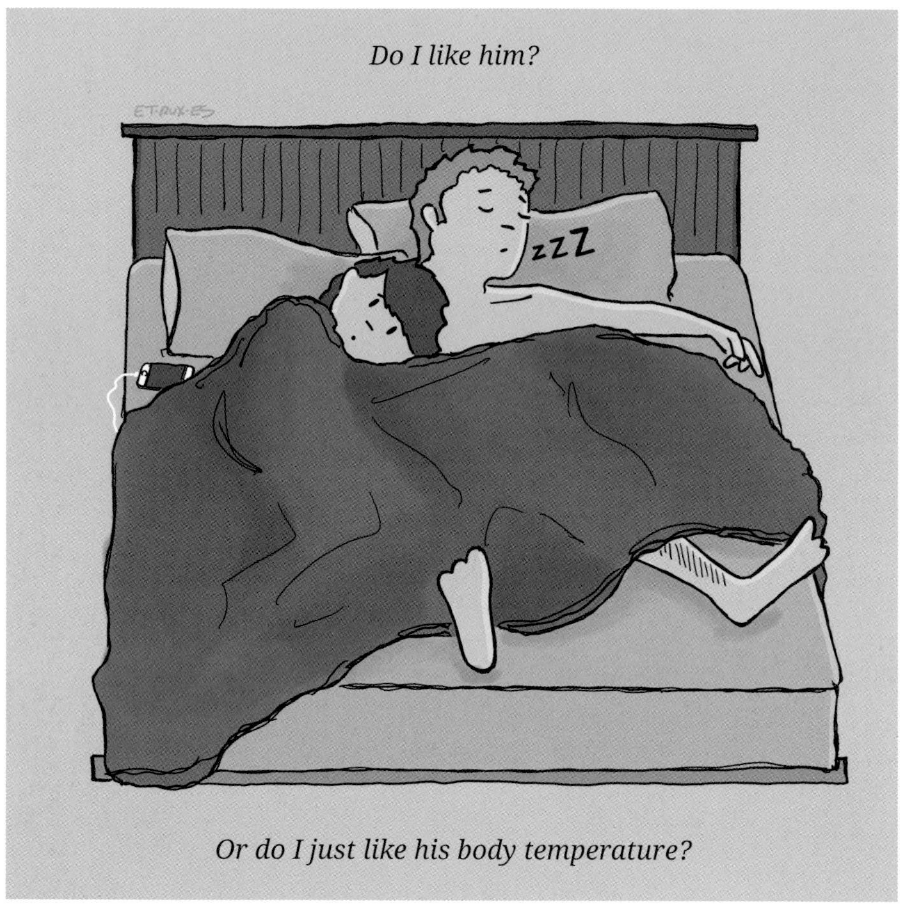
zzZ

Or do I just like his body temperature?

Do I like her?

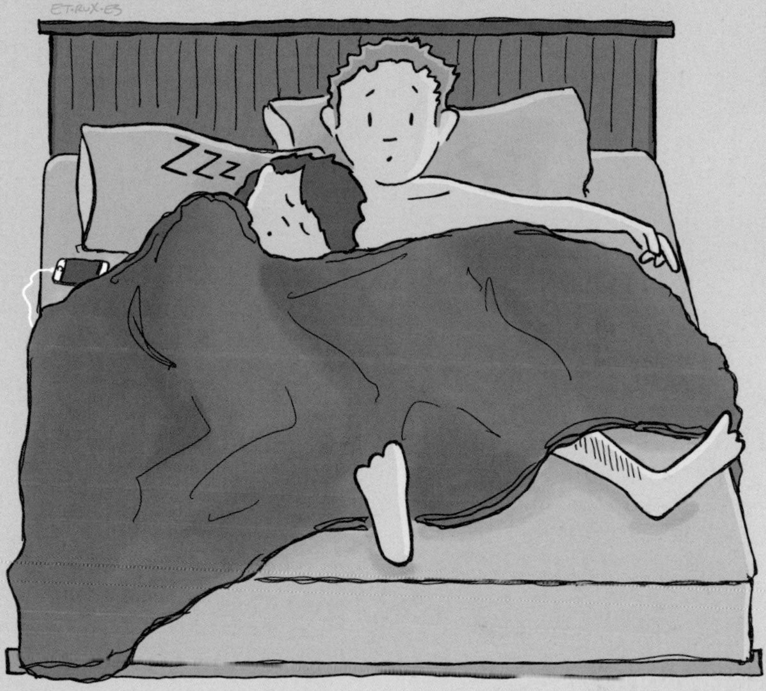
ZZz

Or do I just like her packaging?

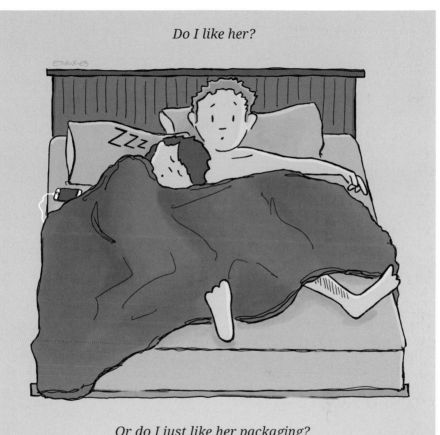

Option A: Ghost him.
Option B: See him again.

"Can you believe they just bought a house together?
That's more official than getting married."

"Now sprinkle some likes in her notifications."

What goes through her head .001 seconds after reading on Bumble that his "real passion is photography."

If your girlfriend says, "Nothing's wrong,"
she's about to kill you.

Or maybe nothing is wrong at all
and you finally found a stable partner.

@trevso_electric

Trying on personalities for the big first date.

If you're on Tinder,
don't be surprised

if you meet the type of people
who would be on Tinder.

@trevso_electric

"Tell me something you haven't already posted on social media."

"Everything was literally going perfect and then we went to the corner store to get water—and he got Aquafina."

"It's been so hard to move on. He had a
washer and dryer literally in his apartment."

"We're at that fun, flirty stage in the relationship
where all we do is tag each other in memes."

"One great thing about being a girl is that you know for certain whether you've had kids or not."

"Slide 1: On March 11, at 11:47 PM EST,
you liked laurenashley1654's selfie."

"Ew, he's calling me. What a psycho."

Generation Why

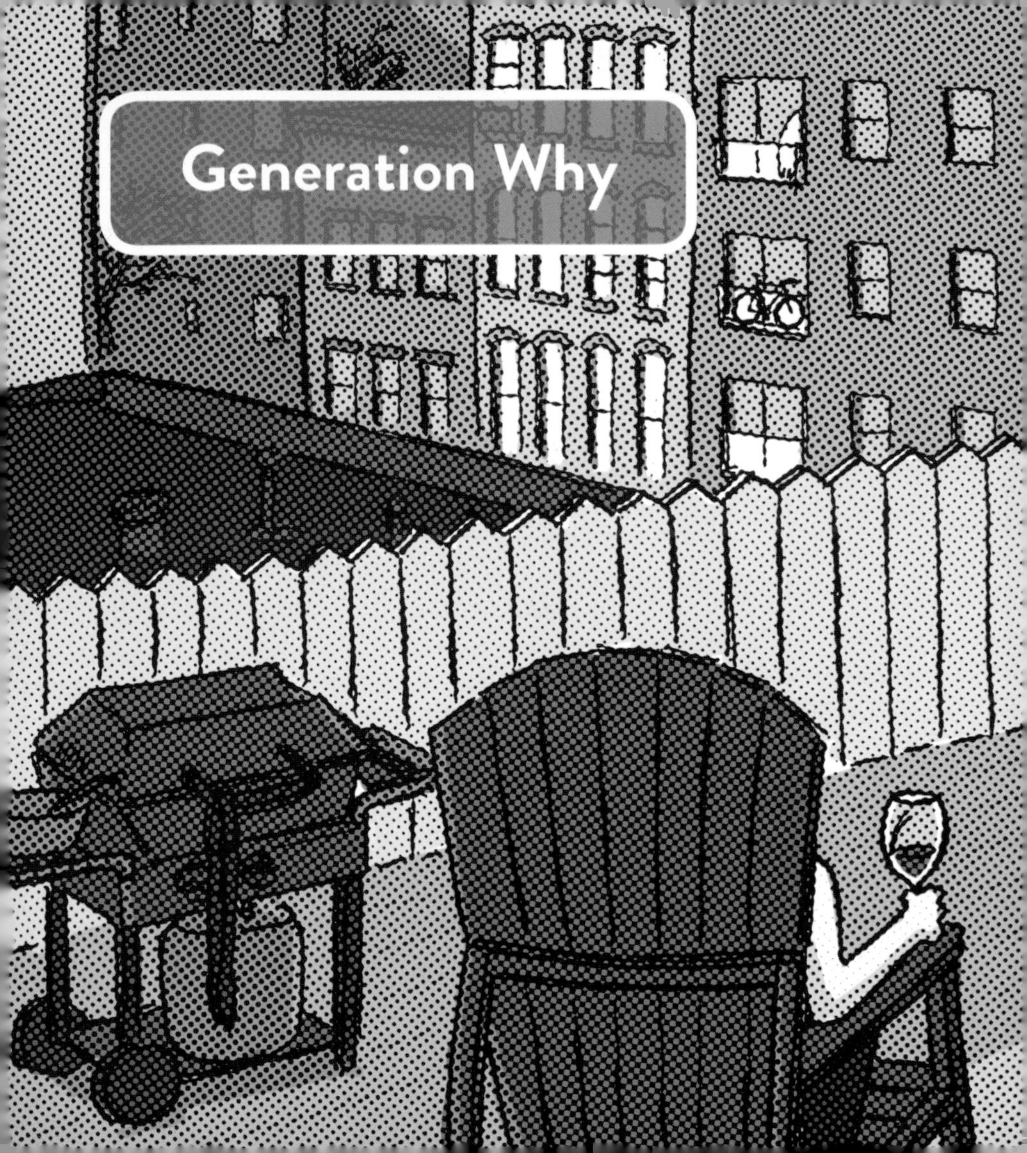

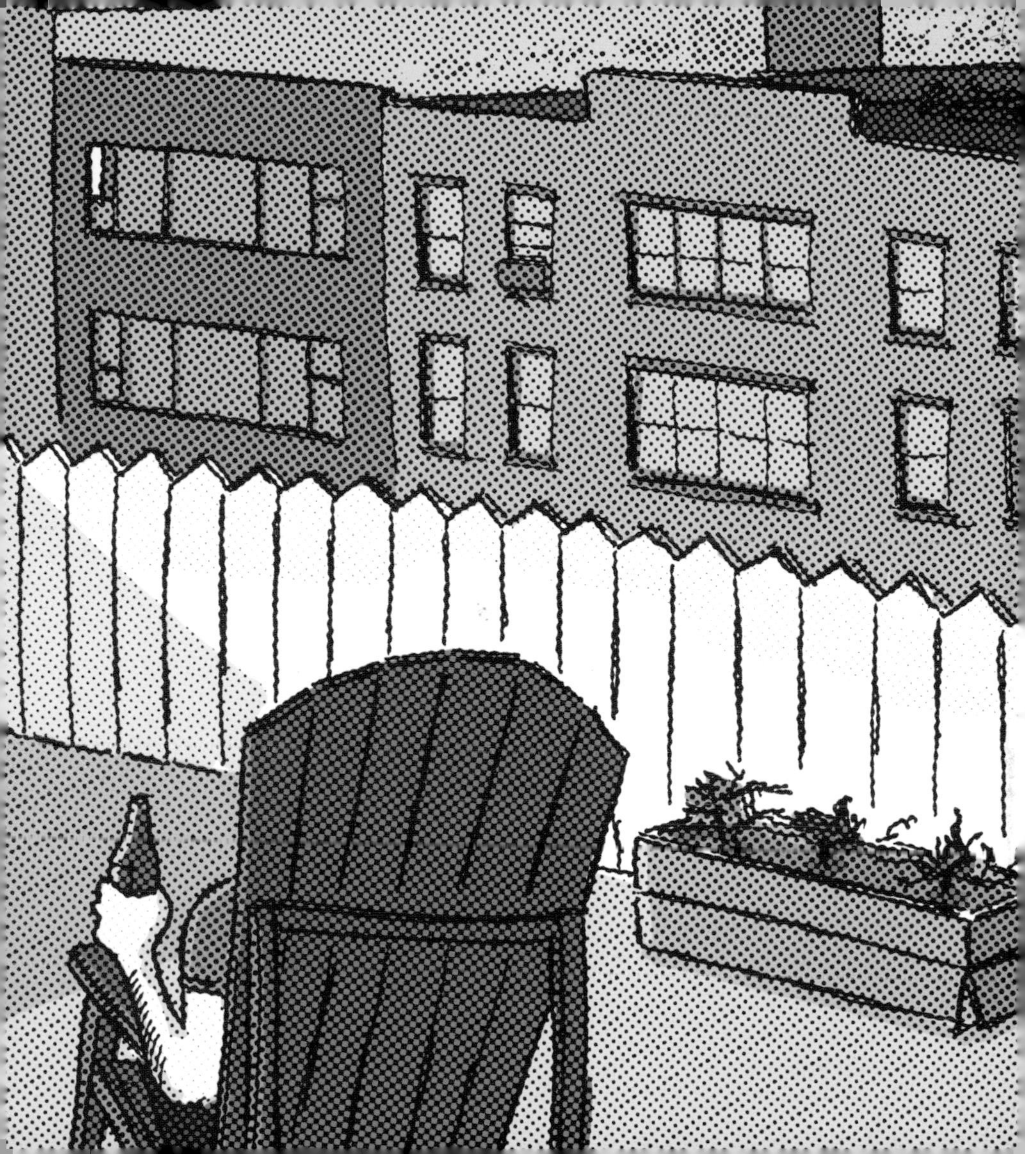

*Started from the middle
now we're struggling*

*to earn a fraction
of what our parents have.*

@trevso_electric

"Let's talk about that all-caps email."

Defying gender stereotypes.

One meal at a time.

"Our only recourse is to redefine 'entitlement' as the millennials' primary character flaw."

*"What you'll love about this apartment
is not defaulting on your student loans."*

@jeremyweissman

"I'm not being modest, I actually suck."

Let's play a game called:
"How to project success when odds are you're a complete failure."

"We discovered this great Korean place.
We were the only white people there."

"What if 'he' identifies outside the gender binary?"

Status update: Saw my doppelgänger on the way home from work. Excited to say I'm happy with my life decisions.

"I'm an adult. I can make my own decisions."

"You're asking where I'm from? Or for the ethnicity of my parents?"

Girl: What if we lived here?

Guy: We'd be so broke.

Girl: But we'd be so happy.

Guy: They say you can't put a price on happiness.

Girl: Actually, you can. $6,400/mo.

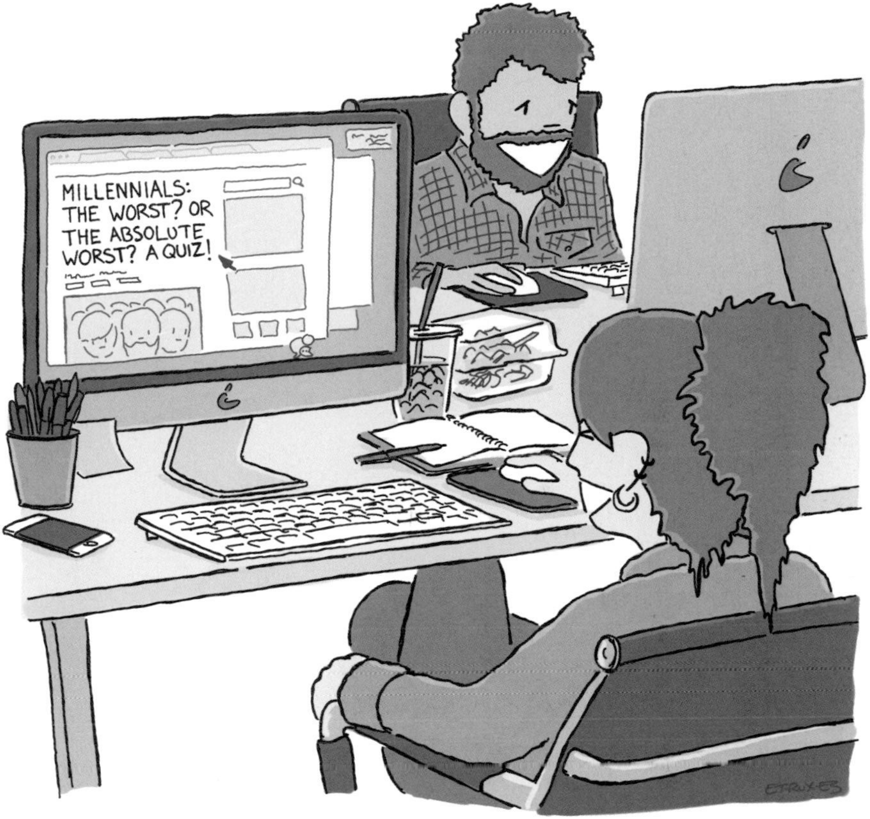
MILLENNIALS: THE WORST? OR THE ABSOLUTE WORST? A QUIZ!

"Will you be checking any privilege with us this afternoon?"

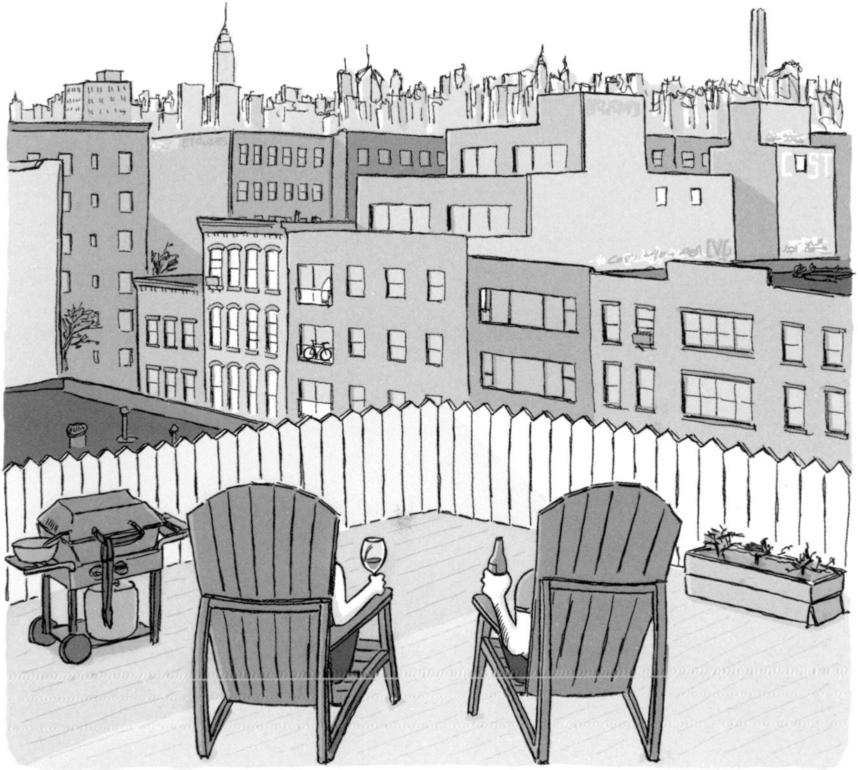

The Dream.

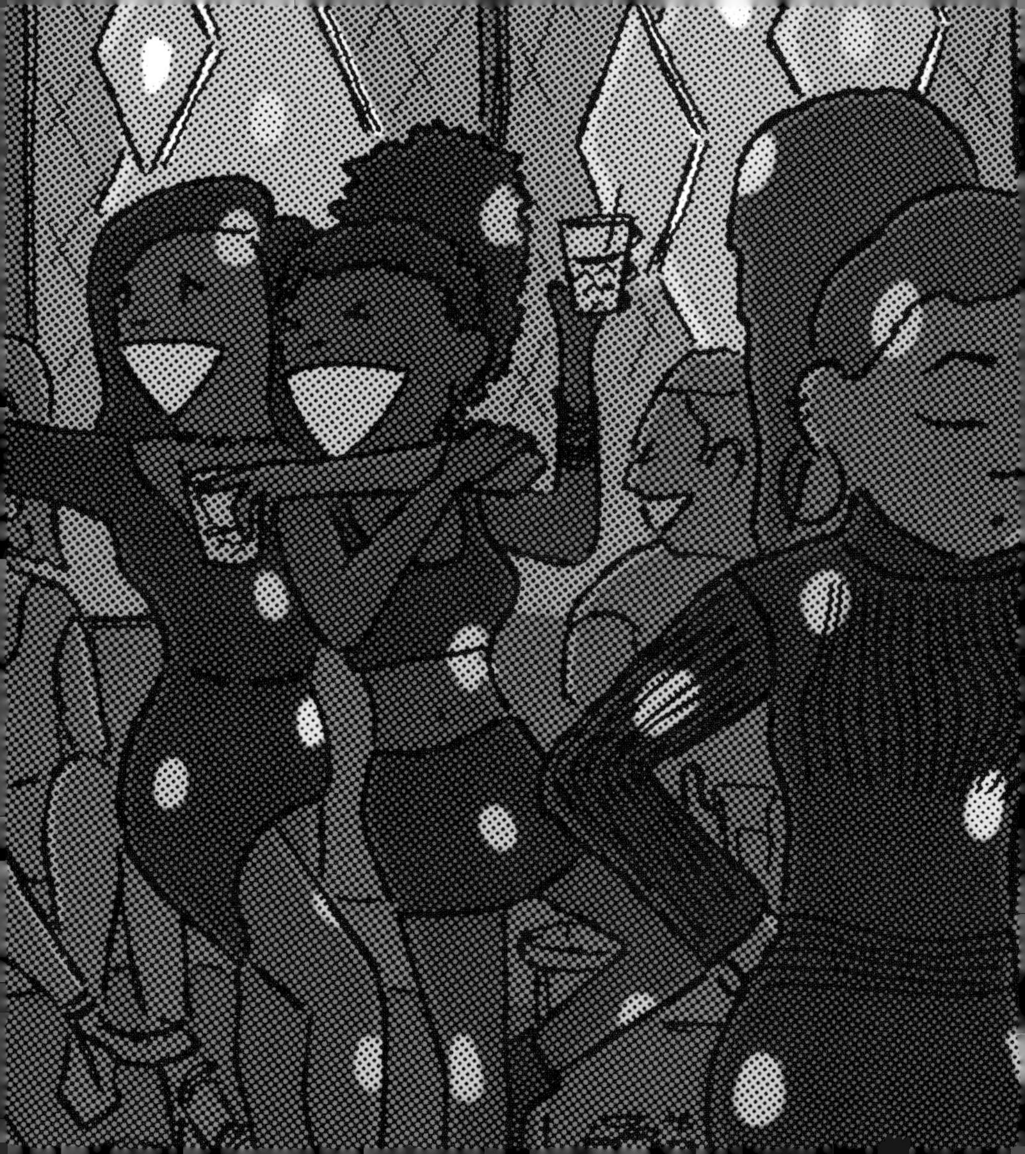

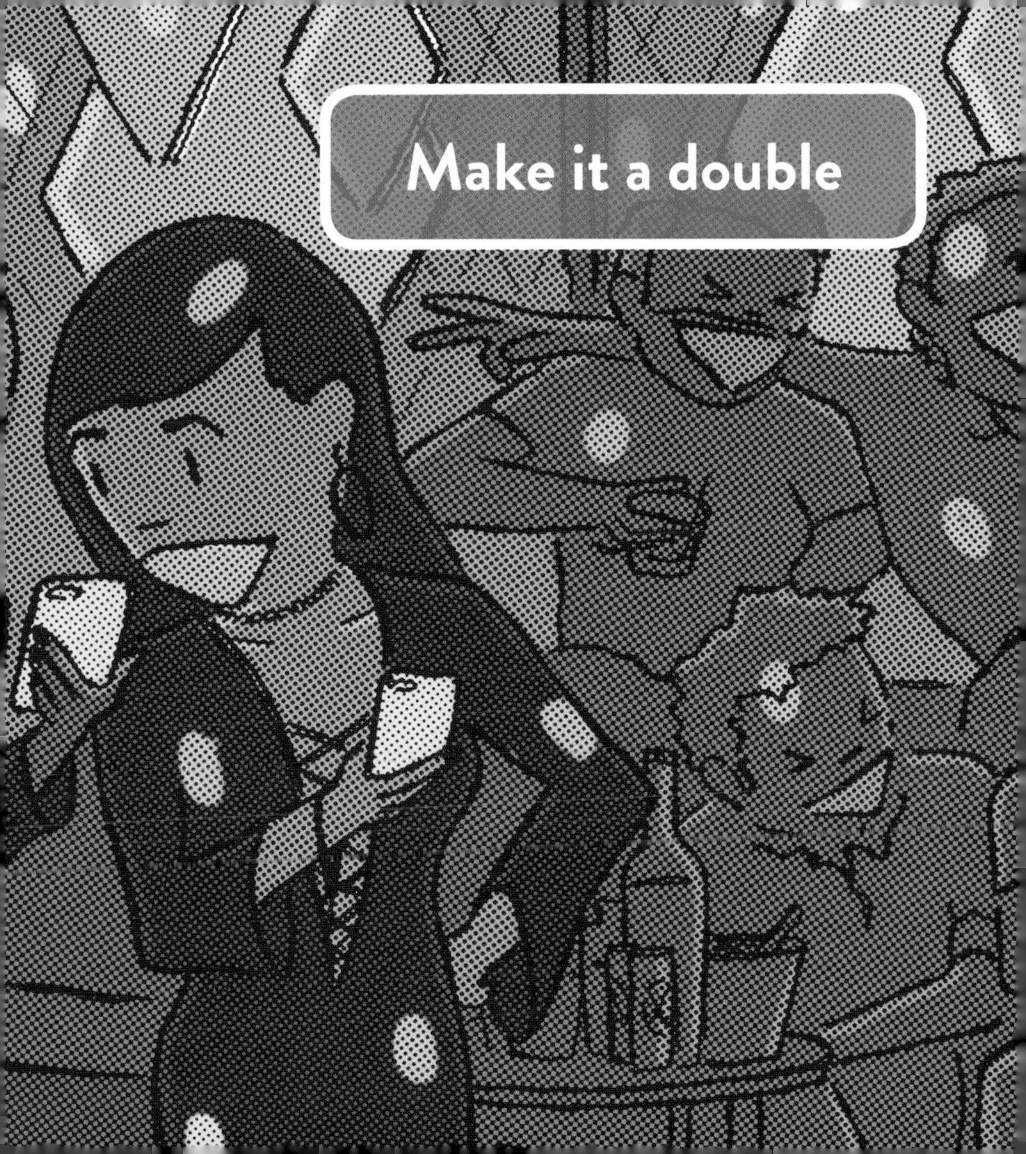
Make it a double

"I'm sorry, but we're cash only."

"I'll meet you guys there, I need to get my steps in."

*"Before we start, everyone sign the NDAs on the counter—
just in case we come up with something brilliant."*

"Pizza won't ignore your texts."

"Let us know when we can start eating."

@nycfoodgals

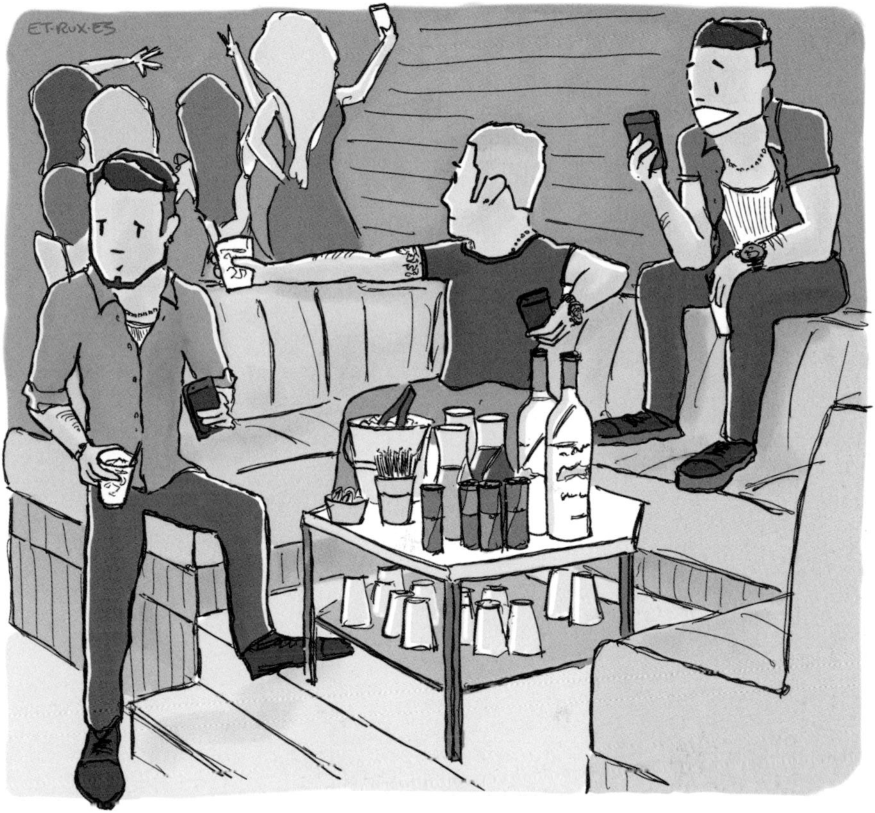

"They'll come, bro."

The Snap story of our lives:

Friday night.   *Saturday morning.*

@ohhmygoddard

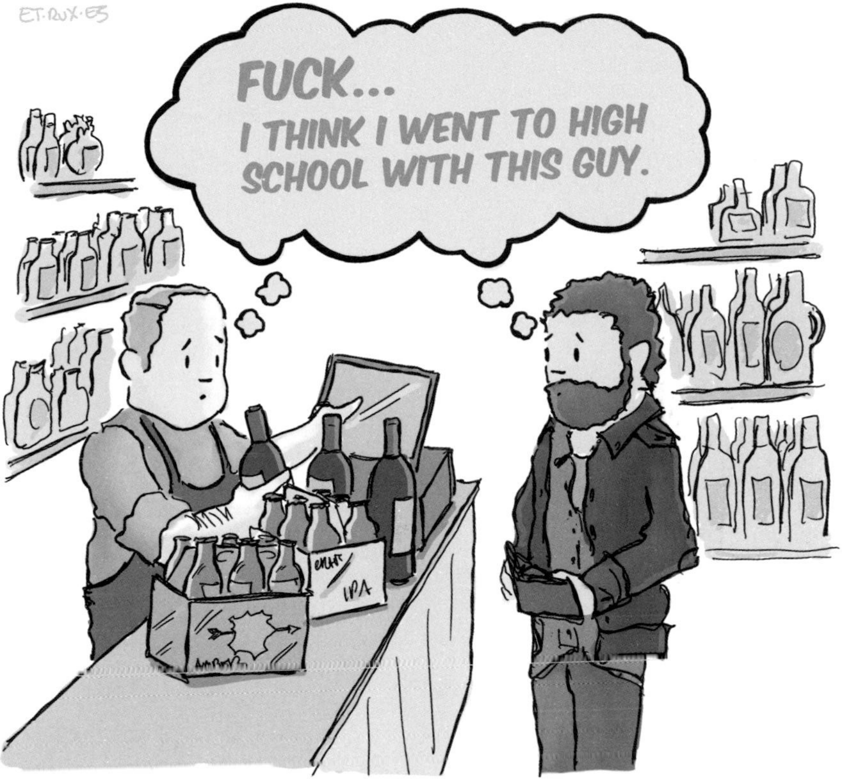
ET·RUX·E5
FUCK...
I THINK I WENT TO HIGH SCHOOL WITH THIS GUY.
IPA

Thanksgiving weekend.

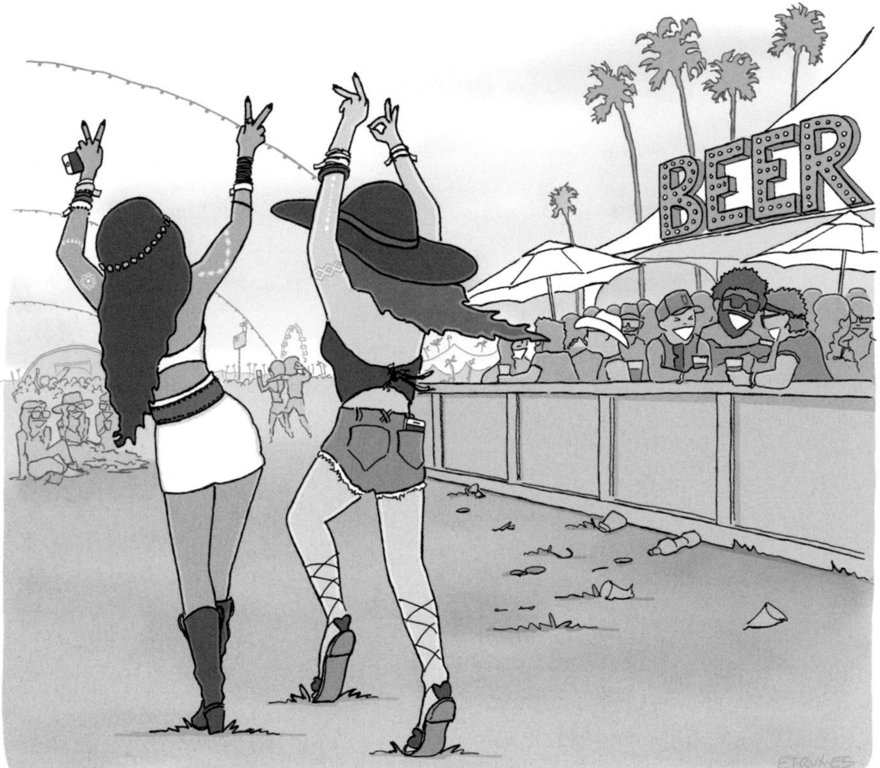
BEER
ETRUX-ES

Molly knows no bounds.

"He keeps screenshotting my Snaps. Is he flirting with me?"

"Sorry, babe, I only bring cash if I'm gonna buy weed."

"Our stories have been so repetitive lately. We need a vacation."

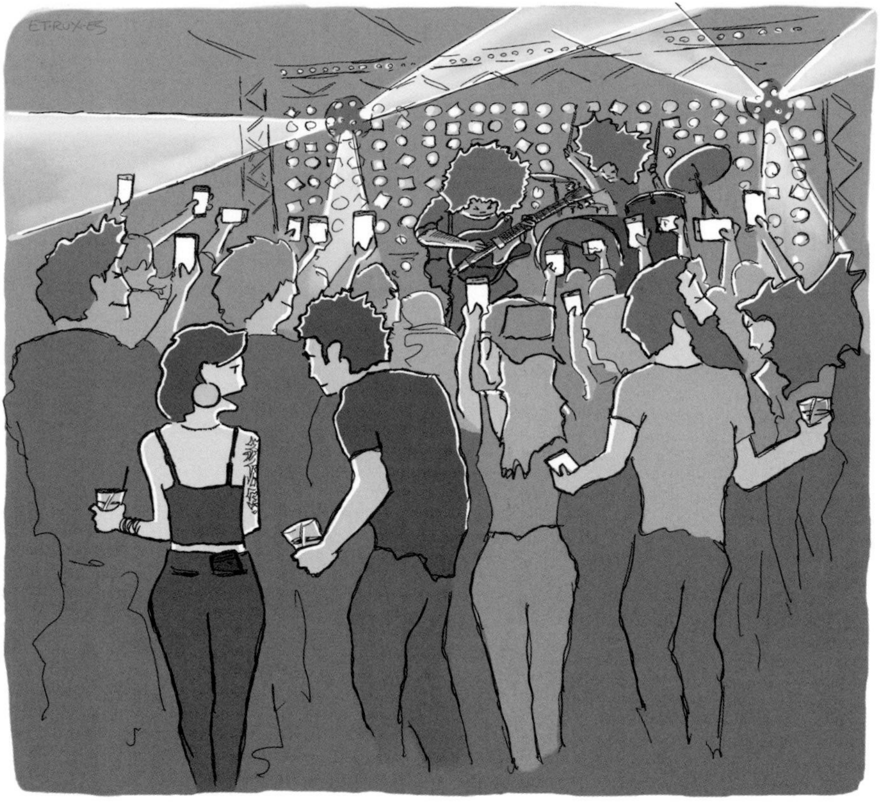

"Let's get out of here."

"Ugh, we're dressing cute tonight?"

Bouncer: Slip me $60 and I'll hook you up.

Guy: What's your Venmo?

"Wait, I smiled, omg, take it again!!"

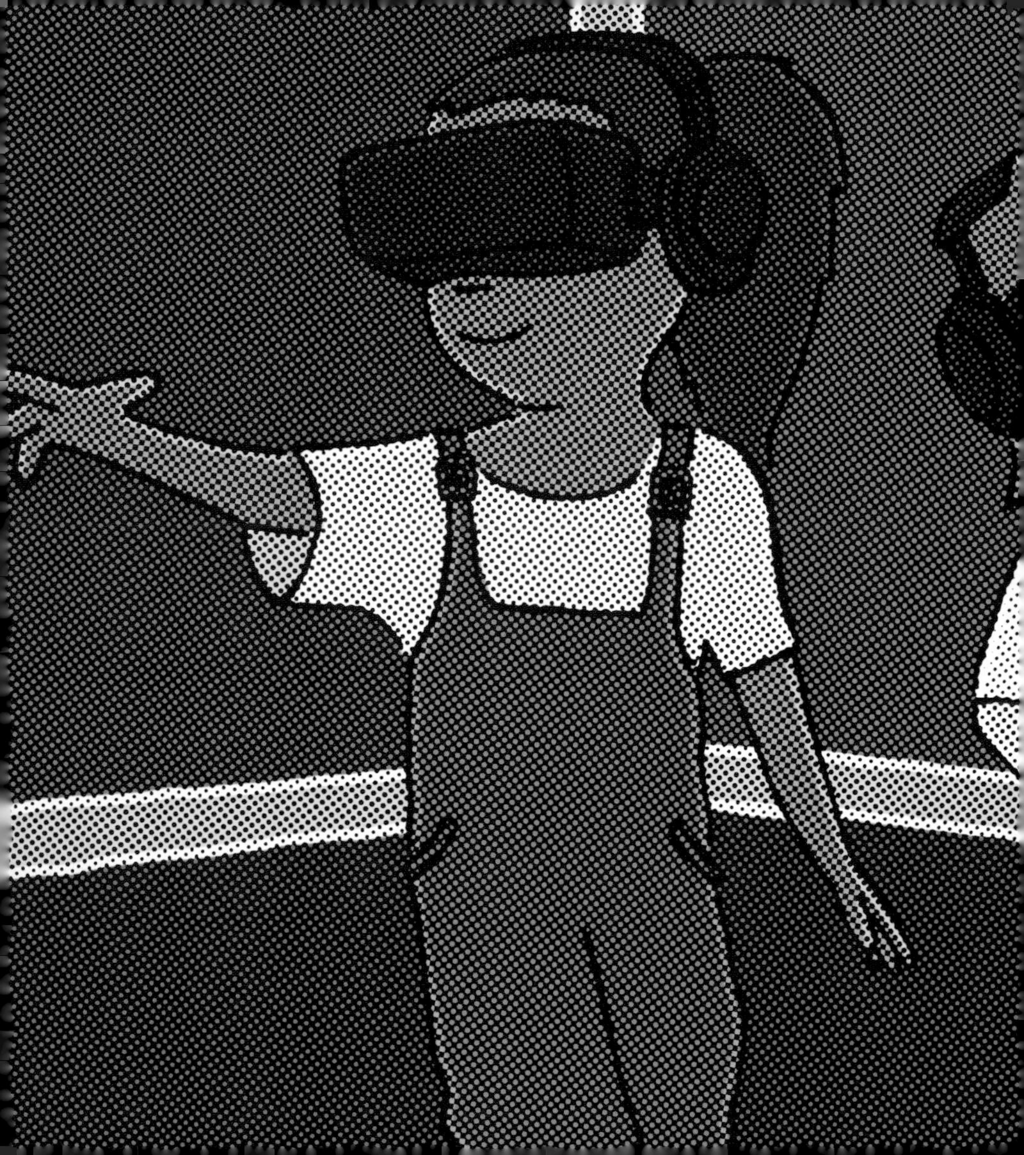

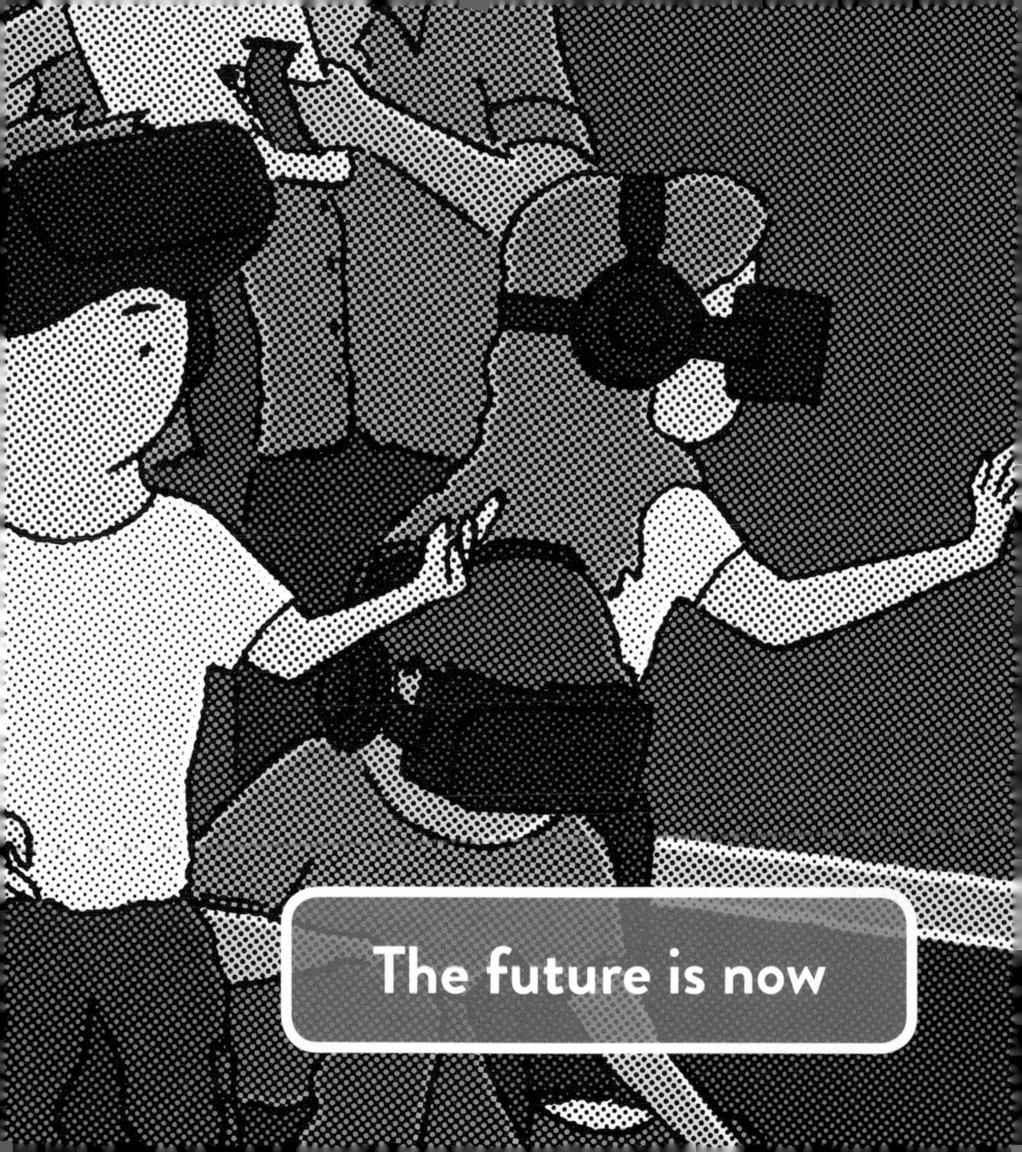
The future is now

"Your baby pics are adorable, but we're not going all the way until I see your genome."

@jeremyweissman

"Someday all this will be waterfront."

"The more we drink at home, the more we save for tickets to Mars."

"He's painting, let's not interrupt his flow."

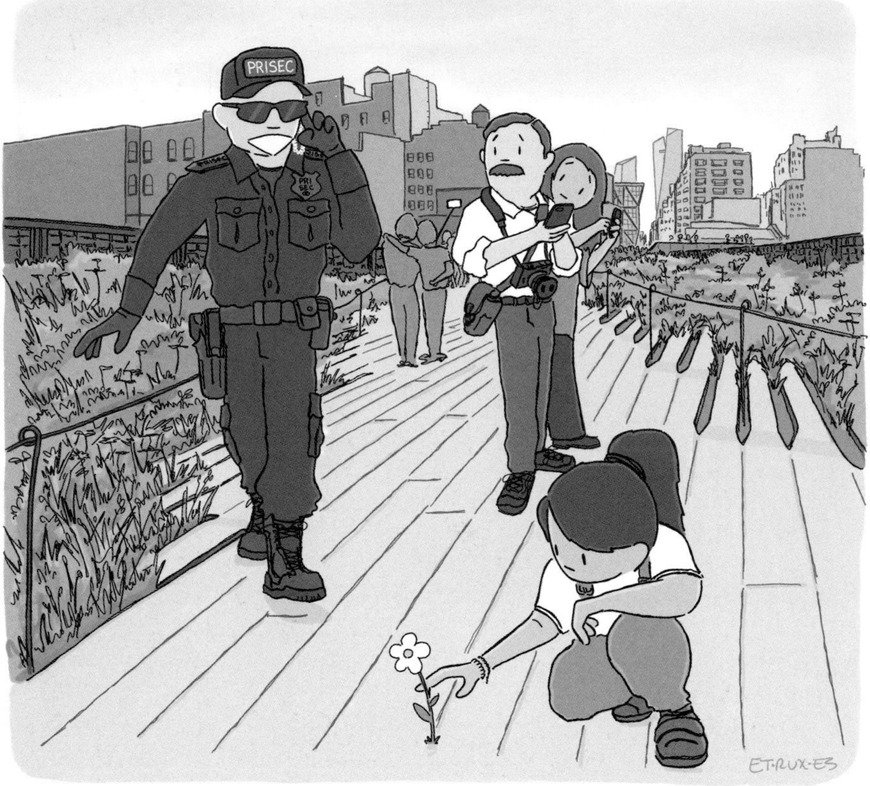
PRISEC
ET·RUX·ES

"I'm sorry, but that's private property."

"Hold up . . . are road sodas allowed in driverless cars?"

Human: Hey Siri, when will artificial intelligence surpass human intelligence and forever change the course of humanity?

Siri: Make sure you don't blow yourselves up first.

Girl 1: Apparently, there are 100 Earth-like planets for every grain of sand in the world. That is insane.

Girl 2: Yeah, but do any of them have Nutella?

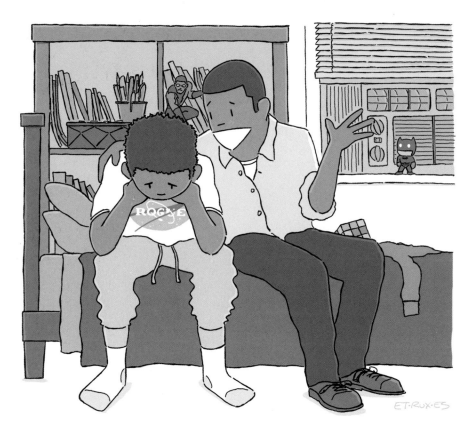

"*Find out what she likes, then program a bot to fire pictures of it at her account twice an hour until she responds.*"

"It's not you. It's your family's carbon footprint."

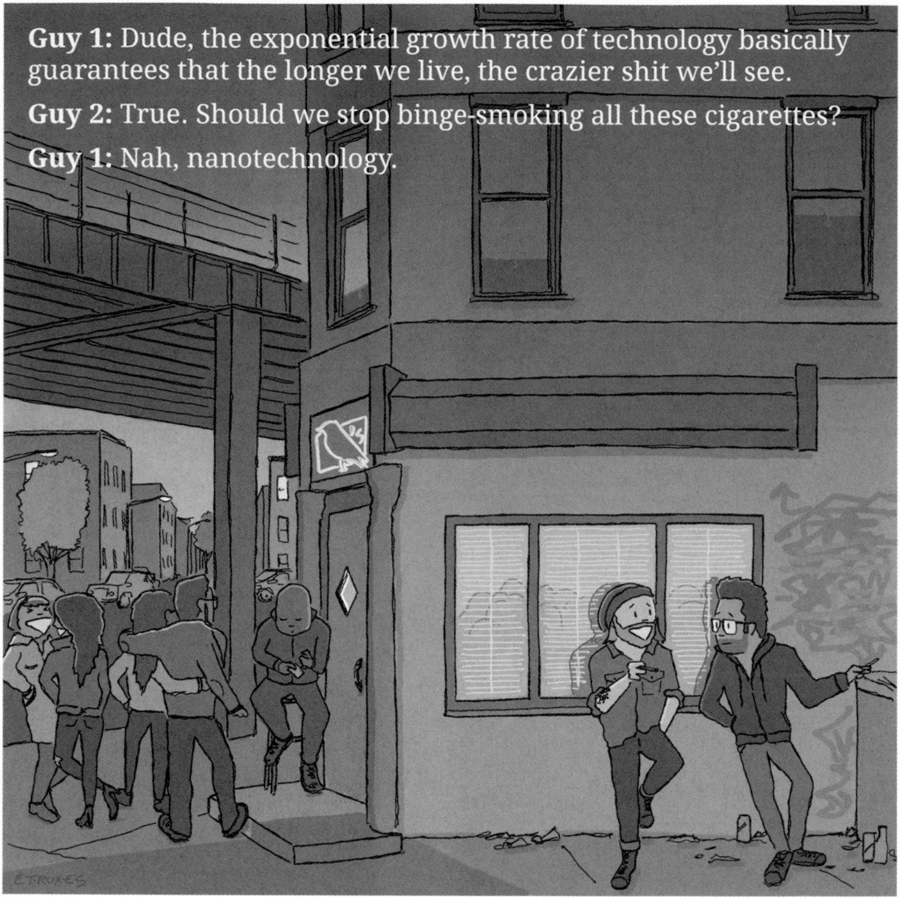
Guy 1: Dude, the exponential growth rate of technology basically guarantees that the longer we live, the crazier shit we'll see.
Guy 2: True. Should we stop binge-smoking all these cigarettes?
Guy 1: Nah, nanotechnology.
E. TROXES

"Man, whoever is running this simulation we're
stuck in sure has a twisted sense of humor."

"This next exhibit is called: 'The World Before the Internet.'"

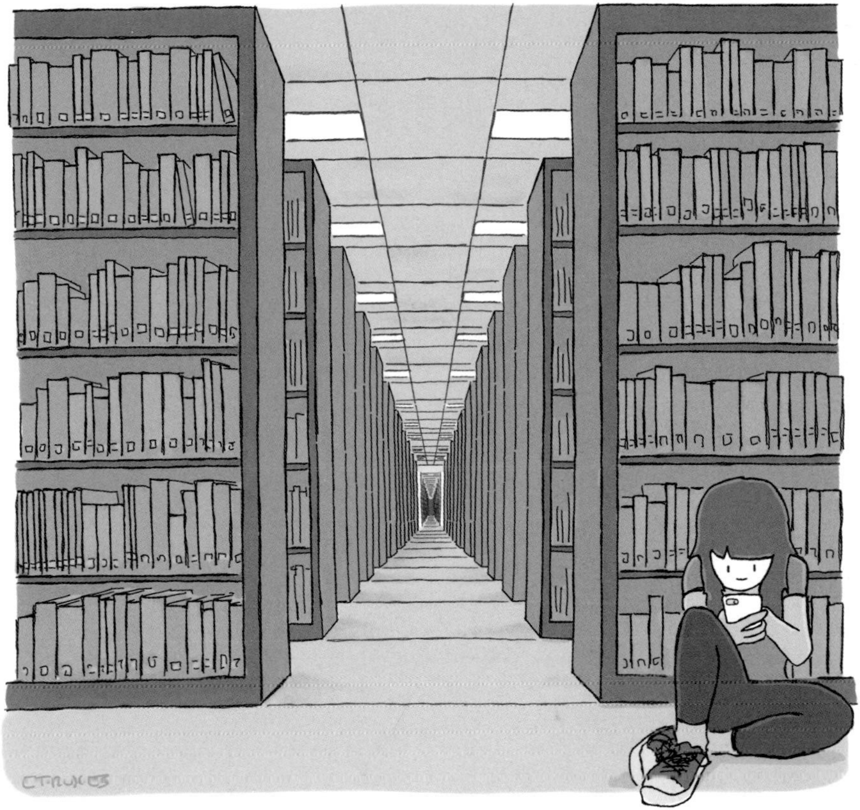

Acknowledgments

I'd like to thank my wife Clementina—*amor de mis amores*—for your unwavering love, patience, support, and helping me see what's always in front of me. *Te dedico este libro.*

To my family: Thomas and An-Ming, for your guidance and years nourishing our creativity; Patrick and Yi-Mei, for your brilliance, clarity, and strategic direction.

A mi otra familia: Carlos, Maria, Axel, Diego, Cristobal, Charlie, *y* Alejandro. *Muchísimas gracias por su apoyo.*

A huge thank you to Andrew Perlmutter at *Green Light Magazine* and Jacob Savage at *The Nassau Weekly*. You are both major players in making this a reality. To my teachers, but especially T. Kelly Wilson and Jennifer Riley, for emphasizing the need to stand still and observe; and to John Nastasi, for the incubation, mentorship, and comedic genius. A special thank you to Tim Donnelly for your killer reporting, and to Jeremy Weissman for your deep dives and keen observations over the years.

Thank you to my followers, and the people behind the accounts I've collaborated with. A special shoutout to @kreativ31 for finding me early, @friendofbae and @tank.sinatra for keeping me going,

@gambles for your many mediums, @ohhmygoddard for repping the target demographic, @overheardla for the synergy, and @trev-so_electric for your brilliance tragically cut short. A special thank you to the family and estate of Trevor Schlingheyde.

To all the friendships over the years, especially: 401/413, BK Varsity, #brooklynorrussia, and our L.A. fam. You guys are brilliant and will always be an inspiration.

To Samantha Weiner and the team at Abrams for making this possible—for your clarity, vision, and putting up with me all this time. We did it! And a very special thank you to Stephanie Delman. You're beyond talented and I'm so honored to be working with you.

For all that is to come.

Credits

A special thank you to the creative individuals behind these accounts for the following collaborations:

@asuspiciouspotato (David Doloboff): 31

@basicbetchproblem (Libby de Leon): 139

@bogartmypix (Alex Howe): 66

@gambles (Matthew Daniel Siskin): 21

@jeremyweissman (Jeremy Weissman): 56, 111, 112, 144, 152

@larkinclark (Larkin Clark): 36, 73, 75

@mytherapistsays: 104

@nycfoodgals: 129, 130

@ohhmygoddard (Shannon Goddard): 13, 17, 79, 83, 85, 132, 135

@overheardla, @overheardnewyork (Jesse Margolis): 14, 19, 34, 84

@tank.sinatra (George Resch): 76, 81

@theyearofelan (Elan Gale): 71

@trevso_electric (Trevor Schlingheyde, RIP): 15, 70, 77, 96, 98, 108

@womenwholovewine: 82